ON YOUR MARK, GET SET, GO!
A Guide for Beginning Physical Education Teachers

Terry A. Senne, Ph.D.
East Carolina University

National Association for Sport and Physical Education
an association of the American Alliance for
Health, Physical Education, Recreation and Dance

1900 Association Drive • Reston, VA 20191
naspe@aahperd.org • 703-476-3410 • www.naspeinfo.org

Dedication
In loving dedication to my family…
Mike & the kids….Kelly, Mic, & Jake

Acknowledgements
Many individuals, through both personal and professional contact, and
life experiences have directly impacted the development of this text. I am
indebted to my family, friends, professional colleagues, former professors,
and students who have mentored and/or influenced me along my journey as a
professional educator. Additionally, I am grateful to NASPE Publications Staff and
the reviewers who offered support, insights, and challenges. Thank you for your
professional contributions to the text.

Craig Buschner, Ed.D.
California State University – Chico

Susan Schwager, Ed.D.
Montclair State University

Deborah Tannehill, Ph.D.
Pacific Lutheran University

Bonnie Tjeerdsma-Blankenship, Ph.D.
Purdue University

Address orders to: AAHPERD Publications, P.O. Box 385, Oxon Hill, MD 20750-0385, call 1-800-321-0789, or
order on line at www.aahperd.org/naspe.
Order Stock No. 304-10264.

Printed in the United States of America.

ISBN 0-88314-745-9

Suggested citation for this book:

Senne, T. A. (2004). *On your mark, get set, go!: A guide for beginning physical education teachers.* Reston, VA:
National Association for Sport and Physical Education.

CONTENTS

PART FOUR   STAYIN' ALIVE: SURVIVAL & DEVELOPMENT

LIST OF FIGURES

LIST OF TABLES

PREFACE

The idea of writing of this book originated during my time as member and chair of NASPE's Council on Professional Preparation in Physical Education (COPPPE). COPPPE was delegated the task of updating a former, well-written NASPE publication, *Transition to Teaching* (Bain & Wendt, 1983). I enthusiastically offered to undertake this task. After review and deliberation, the decision was made to write a new book, rather than revise the former. And thus, *On Your Mark, Get Set, Go! A Guide for Beginning Physical Education Teachers* evolved.

I believe teacher educators lack sufficient time to fully transition teacher candidates as they progress from the university to their first teaching position. I hope this handbook will be of assistance in accomplishing this major metamorphosis. And, although the book is written for beginning physical educators, it is my hope that all teacher educators find a way to get this book into the hands of their teacher candidates prior to graduation—perhaps as a textbook for student teaching seminar or another capstone course within the physical education teacher education program.

For those who've recently accepted your first teaching position, or are in the midst of the job search process, I hope you will find this book truly valuable as you make your way through the sometimes murky, and often challenging, waters of induction. If you keep students as your first and foremost priority, you will be well on your way to providing them with a quality and developmentally appropriate physical education program.

PART I - On Your Mark...

Chapter 1 addresses specific components necessary to secure a teaching position and has been slightly modified from a recent two-part *JOPERD* publication (Senne, 2002a, 2002b). Components addressed are: (a) teaching philosophy, (b) cover letter, (c) resume, (d) references, (e) application process, (f) teaching portfolio as a marketing tool, (g) interview strategies and guidelines, (h) job search techniques, and (i) available resources.

Chapter 1
Transition to Teaching[1]

Preservice physical education teachers and their counterparts in other educational disciplines are often well prepared to assume an initial teaching position in their area of expertise. However, the link so often absent from teacher preparation programs is the component that provides direction and guidance regarding how to secure that first job—or getting your foot in the door. The purpose of this chapter is to provide a clear understanding of the basic components needed to secure that first physical education teaching position. The components addressed include: (a) teaching philosophy, (b) cover letter, (c) resume, (d) references, (e) application process, (f) teaching portfolio as a marketing tool, (g) interview strategies and guidelines, (h) job search techniques, and (i) available resources.

Teaching Philosophy

The teaching philosophy is probably the most difficult piece to develop, but once completed, the rest falls into place. Your teaching philosophy will be reflected throughout the job application process, from development of the resume to the actual job interview itself. Often, teacher candidates developed a skeleton of a philosophy statement as a component of their portfolio. As a key component, it is necessary to ensure that it genuinely reflects your beliefs and assumptions about teaching and learning.

Once written, your teaching philosophy provides a school administrator with a fairly succinct picture of who you are as you prepare to enter the teaching profession. It addresses several aspects (Sprinthall, N., Sprinthall, R., & Oja, 1994). First, a teaching philosophy depicts an individual's beliefs and assumptions about the *goals of physical education*. Within this context, consider the purpose of physical education, its importance, and its overall value within a student's educational program. You may then choose to describe, in basic terms, the general curriculum you envision for your students (i.e., fitness, educational gymnastics and dance, lifetime activities, etc.), as well as any other aspects you find applicable. Several NASPE resources may be of assistance to you in this process. A select number

---

[1]Modified from: Transition to Teaching—Parts 1 & 2/JOPERD Jan/Feb. 2002

of these documents can be found in Table 6., Available Resources, at the end of this chapter.

Second, include a component to address is *how students learn.* This section describes how your teaching style compliments student learning. Do you believe that all students are at the same developmental level in terms of psychomotor, cognitive, and affective competencies? If not, how will you accommodate the diverse needs of your learners? How will you vary the content so that it is developmentally appropriate for all students? How will you attend to the varied learning styles of your students?

Third, address *your role as a physical education teacher.* What does it entail? What do you need to do so that your students receive a quality physical education program? Many NASPE resources can aid in the development of this component as well. What is it that you wish to accomplish as a physical education teacher? What will your students derive from your teaching? What do you believe are your major roles?

Fourth, describe your beliefs and assumptions regarding *behavior management.* Have you developed a behavior management plan that includes rules, protocols, consequences, and motivation techniques to assist you in the development of a productive learning environment for your students? Will all students receive the same consequences? What preventive measures might you employ to reduce the potential for behavior management problems? How can motivational techniques be used to increase appropriate behavior? These are some examples of questions you might respond to as you develop this particular section of your teaching philosophy.

Last, incorporate your beliefs about *grading and assessment* in physical education. How will you assess your students? Will you use traditional or authentic forms of assessment, or a combination of both? Is it important to assess in all three learning domains (psychomotor, cognitive, and affective)? What specific grading components will you use? How much will each grading component be weighted? If you can answer these questions, you should be able to tackle this component with ease.

A few suggestions are in order as you proceed to write your teaching philosophy. Initially, it might be best to list each of the above components, and then jot down (in bulleted format) items that come to mind as you reflect on each category. Once you have several bullets under a single category, attempt to write that component in paragraph format. Attack one component at a time until you've addressed all five areas. It will be to your benefit to boldface or underline each of the five major philosophy components within the teaching philosophy statement. This will allow the reader to preview aspects of primary interest, without the need to read the teaching philosophy in its entirety. Next, reread the document to ensure that it clearly states your beliefs and assumptions about teaching and learning. If there are one or more key aspects not currently reflected in one of the five previous categories, you might wish to add an *additional comments* section. Delete any "I believe" or "I feel" statements. These statements are already implied, since you are writing *your* philosophy. Modify and adjust as necessary. The length of the teaching philosophy statement is dependent upon what you have to say. State your beliefs as clearly and concisely as possible.

If desired, your philosophy statement may be included as a part of your teaching application materials. Alternatively, it becomes a great tool to use as you address specific questions during the interview process.

Cover Letter

The cover letter is a very important step in securing your first teaching position. It is the first contact with a potential school system. It serves as a scaffold between the vacancy listing and your resume. It is your "sales pitch" for the teaching position and your first attempt to "get your foot in the door." Consequently, a good cover letter may make the difference in whether you are selected to interview for the teaching position. The cover letter includes three major sections: (a) the introduction, (b) the body or "the sell," and (c) the closing (Wallencheck, 1998). Refer to the sample cover letter provided in Figure 1.

Figure 1. Sample Cover Letter

Dr. John Smith, Director of Personnel
Central County Public Schools
Central City, NC xxxxx

Dear Dr. Smith:

Introduction

Please accept this as a letter of application for the Central City Middle School physical education teaching vacancy posted on the *Troops to Teachers* website. I am currently completing my final weeks of student teaching, and will be graduating in May with a B.S. degree in Physical Education (Teacher Preparation). My career objective is to gain employment as a middle school physical education teacher and coach.

The "Sell"

My student teaching experience at Johnson Middle School is both rewarding and challenging. I learned a great deal during the last several years, and have honed my skills in teaching particularly well during this final semester. I truly enjoy working with middle school students, and feel that I interact very well with this age group. I taught a variety of instructional units including fitness and conditioning, speedball, badminton, and recreational dance during my student teaching experience. I also served as the assistant volleyball coach for the 7th grade girls' volleyball team, and gained a tremendous amount of knowledge and planning experience in the process.

Continuing professional development is an important aspect of the teaching profession, and I regularly take advantage of opportunities to enhance my knowledge and development in the field of physical education. During the past three years, I attended the state NCAAHPERD Convention and numerous workshops in fitness and dance. Currently, I serve as President of the EXSS Majors' Club at Southeastern University. I believe these professional develop-ment and leadership experiences have prepared me well for the role of teaching in physical education.

Closing

Enclosed please find my resume and completed teaching application materials for your review. I am sincerely interested in this teaching position, and will be available to interview at your earliest convenience. If further information is needed, please contact me at (252) 555-1212 between 4:00 and 7:00 PM. I look forward to hearing from you very soon.

Sincerely,

Student A. Teacher

Enclosures

The *introductory paragraph* is brief and to the point. It provides two pieces of information. First, it specifies the position for which you are applying, as well as the source of the vacancy listing (i.e., newspaper, website, vacancy post-ing at a college/university, job fair). Second, it addresses why you are applying for the position. This will set the stage for the body of the cover letter.

The *body* of the cover letter can be looked upon as the sell. This is where you make a case for why you are qualified for the advertised position. This section serves primarily to highlight and market your most important qualifications and pertinent accomplishments. Although most credentials will be visible within your resume, use this section of the cover letter to draw attention to those qualifications that make you most suitable for the position. As you write this section, it is critical to carefully align your qualifications with the responsibilities outlined within the vacancy listing. For example, if the teaching position requires that you assume coaching responsibilities, it will be important for you to discuss prior coaching experience, as well as how it complements the extracurricular responsibilities addressed in the job listing. This section of the cover letter is approximately one to two paragraphs in length, thus allowing sufficient space for you to address your most pertinent qualifications.

Lastly, bring the cover letter to *closure*. Two items should be addressed within this final section of the cover letter. First, provide contact information and indicate when you will be available to interview. Generally, it is a good idea to state you are available to interview "at their convenience." The contact information provides phone numbers where you can be reached, as well as times that you will be available for contact. Second, make note of any enclosures to be submitted with the cover letter. These may include, but are not limited to: (a) the application itself, (b) resume, (c) references, and (d) other pertinent materials.

Since the cover letter is actually the first impression you make on the school system as a candidate for the particular teaching position, make it a *lasting impression*. Carefully check the cover letter to ensure that it is appropriately worded, concise, and error free. In general, a cover letter should be no more than one page in length. Administrators are more likely to read it thoroughly if it is brief and to the point.

Resume

The third component to develop in preparation for securing your first teaching position is the resume. A resume depicts a brief, yet concise, summary of your education and experience. As such, the length of the resume is limited to one to two pages maximum. The resume is easy to read, and provides the employer with the ability to quickly glance and locate specific types of information regarding your qualifications. Many different resume formats exist; however, most require similar types of information. For an individual seeking a teaching position, the following components should be addressed in the resume: (a) personal data, (b) career objective, (c) education, (d) teaching/professional experience, (e) certifications/specialized skills, (f) other work experience, (g) honors/activities, (h) professional organizations, and (i) references (Coleman, 1998). These

Figure 2. Sample Resume

Student A. Teacher

xxx W. First Street
Any City, NC xxxxx

Phone: (xxx) xxx-xxxx
sat1111@email.edu

Career Objective	To gain employment as a middle school physical education teacher and coach.
Education	**Southeastern University**, Any City, NC (1997-2001) • Bachelor of Science in Physical Education, Teacher Preparation • Minor: General Science • Cumulative GPA: 3.45 (4.0 scale)
Professional Experience	**Internship,** Johnson Middle School, Any Town, NC (spring 2001) • Taught physical education, grades 6-8 (fitness & conditioning, speedball, badminton, and recreational dance) • Evaluated student learning in physical education **Assistant Volleyball Coach**, Johnson Middle School, Any Town, NC (spring 2001) • Assisted with all coaching duties for 7th grade girls' volleyball team **Volunteer Special Olympics Coach**, Greenville, NC (2/00-4/00) • Served as track and field coach (field events)
Certifications & Specialized Skills	NC Initial Teaching Licensure, Physical Education, K-12 (expected 6/01) American Red Cross Community CPR & First Aid
Other Work Experience	**Wal-Mart**, Any City, NC (1998-2001) • Worked as a cashier and in customer service
Honors & Activities	Dean's List (1998-2001) Attended NCAAHPERD State Convention (1998-2001)
Professional Organizations	**EXSS Majors Club,** *President,* Southeastern University (2000-01) **NCAAHPERD**, *Member,* (1998-Present)
References	B. Jane Johnson, Ph.D. Southeastern University, Dept. of EXSS xxx Sports Complex Any City, NC xxxxx Phone: (xxx) xxx-xxxx E-mail: bjjohnson@xxxx.edu

are the minimal components to be addressed. There may be additional components you desire to incorporate as well, some of which are discussed in the following paragraphs. Refer to the sample resume provided in Figure 2.

Typically, the resume will begin with the personal data section. This is usually positioned at the top of the first page of the resume, often serving as the header. It includes name, address, phone number, and e-mail address, if applicable. Following personal data information, it is suggested that a horizontal line be used to separate the remaining components of the resume. The "Career Objective" is the first section following the personal data component. This consists of a one-sentence statement reflecting the type of teaching position you are seeking, as well as any specific types of extracurricular duties you may wish to pursue.

The "Education" section logically follows. Within this section, list your degree (i.e., B.S. in Physical Education), the institution granting the degree, years of attendance, any minor, and, if desired, cumulative GPA. If you attended more than one institution in the completion of your degree, the institution granting the degree should be listed first, followed in chronological order (most recent first) by the additional institutions attended. In some instances, individuals will also choose to indicate their teaching certification within this section.

"Teaching/Professional Experience" is often positioned following the education section. List all prior experience in this section chronologically, beginning with the most recent. If seeking your first teaching position, at least provide your student teaching experience within this section. Other possibilities include prior teaching practicum experiences, coaching experience, athletic training experience, and so forth. These experiences should relate directly to the career objective stated previously in your resume.

"Certifications/Specialized Skills" provides information that details certifications held and/or any specialized skills you possess. Your teaching certification is listed here, along with subject(s) and grade levels for which you are qualified to teach, in addition to the state granting teacher licensure. Perhaps you are also certified in athletic training, lifeguard training, CPR, or in some other specialized skill. If so, it is appropriate to provide that information within this section. Several states also have various coaching certification programs, and if you are a recipient of this type of training, it can be documented here as well.

"Other Work Experience" is exactly as the section heading denotes. Any prior work experience not related to your professional career objective is listed here. This section may include both paid and volunteer work experience, or you may choose to list volunteer experience as a separate category of its own. Once again, list positions chronologically from the most recent.

The "Honors/Activities" section of the resume will document any honors received over the course of your collegiate program (i.e., Dean's List, Honor Roll, Phi Kappa Phi Honor Society). In addition, any extracurricular activities deemed appropriate can also be reported in this section. Perhaps you are a member of an athletic team or intramural team at your college/university. Do you belong to a fraternity, sorority, or some other service organization? Maybe you've attended a state or the national AAHPERD Convention & Exposition. If so, it is appropriate to include that type of information within this category. Or, you may consider adding a separate category to your resume entitled, "Professional Development."

The "Professional Organizations" section of your resume consists of a listing of all professional-type organizations of which you are an active member or officer. Do you belong to a majors club at your college/university? Are you a member of your state and/or national AAHPERD? Perhaps you're a member of a state coaching association. These and comparable organizations are listed within this particular section of the resume.

The "References" section serves as the final resume section. Some individuals will choose to use the following blanket statement, "References available upon request." Nonetheless, it is suggested to list references rather than using the above statement. Listing specific references provides employers with immediate contact information. This will expedite the administrative review process. Include as much contact information as possible for each reference. Minimally, include the names, addresses, and phone numbers of three references. If available, include e-mail addresses as well.

As stated previously, the format design is up to you. A few guidelines will help as you begin this process. Increase and decrease font size to denote various levels within each resume section. Avail yourself of the variety of typefaces available as well. Bullets also can be used to highlight information within certain sections. Use a 10-point font size or larger within the resume document. Additionally, within each section, position contents chronologically, beginning with the most current. Include dates of service as applicable. Hopefully you've kept accurate records (i.e., dates of employment). One of the keys to a good resume is to remain consistent in format throughout the document. Carefully edit and check spelling. Once completed, it is a good idea to save your resume document on a floppy disk, or comparable device. Consequently, it will be easy to add to and update as you accumulate additional experience over time.

References

References refer to individuals who are knowledgeable regarding your teaching qualifications and competencies, as well as additional duties for which you are responsible (career objective). They are able to speak to your qualifications, as well as provide an accurate judgment on your potential for success. There are several sources from which to access appropriate references including your clinical/cooperating teacher(s), university supervisor(s), professors, coaches, school administrators, to name a few. To determine if an individual is qualified to serve as a reference, ask yourself the following questions: (a) Is the individual knowledgeable with respect to my qualifications and competencies? (b) Have I had past difficulties or differences with the individual? (c) Will the individual write a positive recommendation? (Simkins, 1998)

To assist in the process of securing appropriate references, the following may serve as guidelines (refer to Table 1). First, secure references prior to completing student teaching. This enables increased accessibility to individuals from whom you wish to secure a reference. Second, choose references carefully. Consider a variety of reference sources that best represent your abilities and competencies. Third, request the recommendation in person if possible, and provide the individual with ample time to complete the reference. And, always request permission in advance when listing individuals as references in your resume as well. Fourth, supply a pre-addressed, stamped envelope for references to be submitted under separate cover from the application. It is generally a good idea to provide a copy of your resume to the person completing the reference form. This allows him/her the opportunity to review your qualifications and competencies. He or she may choose to

Table 1. Guidelines to Secure References

- Complete *prior to* end of internship (accessibility)
- Choose references carefully
- Consider a variety of reference sources to best represent your abilities/ competencies
- Request recommendation in person
- Allow sufficient time for completion
- Provide pre-addressed, stamped envelope
- Provide a copy of your resume
- Determine whether to request a copy of reference
- Write thank-you note, once received
- Maintain up-to-date references

cite selected items from your resume as he or she completes the reference form/letter. Additionally, you may wish to request a copy of the reference form/letter for your own files; however, this is not usually necessary. Some reference forms will require teacher candidates to identify whether they wish to waive or retain rights to access the reference form. This is an individual preference to be made by the teacher candidate. Some believe it is best to have the reference remain confidential, while others suggest that individuals should never relinquish their rights to view their files. Once you've confirmed receipt of the completed reference, it is suggested that you send the individual a short thank-you note. Finally, take care to maintain up-to-date references in your placement file.

Career services' role in the establishment of a "credentials or placement file" for a college/university graduate is in a transition period, primarily due to advancements in technology. Most now have well-developed websites where a great deal of information can be accessed. Several no longer maintain credential/placement files; but rather, place the responsibility for the maintenance of the file upon the graduate. Regardless of the procedure employed by your specific career services office, it is recommended that you visit their office and/or check out their website at least one semester prior to graduation, availing yourself of services that may be of benefit with respect to landing your first teaching position.

Application Process

The application process can be overwhelming if good organizational and management skills are not employed. Therefore, this section addresses

Table 2. Application and Hiring Process
Step 1 – Search and locate teaching vacancies
Step 2 – Request teaching applications
Step 3 – Submit cover letter, resume, and completed application
Step 4 – Submit reference letters/forms
Step 5 – Request teaching credential file to be sent (career services/placement office)
Step 6 – Confirm receipt of all teaching application materials, credentials, and references
Step 7 – Wait while school system reviews applications and selects interview candidates
Step 8 – Conduct interviews and rank candidates
Step 9 – Accept/reject teaching offer
Step 10 – Sign teaching contract
Step 11 – Approve teacher contract via Board of Education

the application and hiring process, guidelines for completing the application form, and strategies for managing teaching applications. First, it will be beneficial to develop an understanding of the application and hiring process. The application process itself entails several steps. These may vary slightly from one school system to the next, but overall, they provide a fairly succinct overview of the process in general. Table 2 provides a summary of the application and hiring process.

The first step involved in the application process involves searching and locating teaching vacancies. Search techniques will be detailed later within the chapter (see "Job Search Techniques") and therefore, will not be addressed at this time. The second step includes requesting teaching applications from selected school systems that you are interested in pursuing. This can be done through several formats including: (a) request in writing, (b) request by phone, and (c) request via the Internet (e-mail). During step three, the teacher candidate submits a cover letter, resume, and the completed application to the specific school system.

Submission of reference letters/forms denotes the fourth step in the application process. Submission of references for the teacher candidate tends to vary from school system to school system. Some school systems send reference forms to the applicant, along with the application itself. If so, the applicant will be requested to either return the completed reference forms with his or her application, or the reference form may be submitted directly by the individual completing it. Alternatively, contact information for references is provided on the teaching application form. Once received, the school system requests a completed reference form from those individuals listed on the candidate's application. And, the completed reference form is subsequently submitted directly to the school system.

Next, the teacher candidate requests his or her college/university teaching credentials (transcripts, etc.) be submitted to the specific school system, if applicable (step five). Again, this process may vary, dependent upon the institution. Typically, this ends the paperwork portion of the application process.

Following a sufficient period of time, it is suggested that the teacher candidate confirm receipt of all teaching application materials, credentials, and references submitted to the particular school system (step six). This can be easily accomplished with a phone call. Concurrently, you may inquire as to the status of the position for which you applied. Are they still accepting applications? Has the review of applications begun? How far along is the school system in the interview process? While bringing closure to your phone conversation, reinforce and reaffirm your interest in the position.

When the school system deadline for receiving applications arrives, school administrators begin the review process to select teacher candidates they wish to interview. This is the seventh step of the application process. Step eight is the actual interview itself. This step will be addressed in further detail within the "Interview Strategies and Guidelines" section. As the interview process is completed, administrators will rank teacher candidates in terms of first, second, and third choices. Subsequently, the first choice candidate will be contacted and offered the position. Step nine is the accept/reject decision of the teacher candidate; whereby the candidate carefully considers advantages and limitations of the recently offered position. He or she then decides to accept or reject the offer. If the candidate elects to accept the offer, he or she will sign a teaching contract with the school system (step ten). The eleventh and final step in the process occurs when the Board of Education provides final approval through confirmation of the selected teacher candidate for hire.

There are several guidelines for completing the teaching application that may prove beneficial as you initiate this process. Many of these are related to writing mechanics. First, take your time completing the application. Read the entire application through prior to starting. This provides a complete picture of all the information that must be addressed. And, before beginning to write the application itself, photocopy the document and complete your working draft on the photocopy. If the application requests information that does not apply to you specifically, write "N/A" in the space provided. Additionally, be selective when listing previous jobs and volunteer work. Select those most applicable for the specific position for which you are applying. Your resume will provide an excellent resource for you to refer to as you complete the application.

Once the working draft is completed, seek out an individual other than yourself who can proofread the application by checking for possible errors. Similar to the cover letter and resume, the application represents you; therefore, ensuring an error-free document is critical. After the application has been proofed for errors, write the final copy for submission. Type or print the application legibly. If printing, use black ink. Some school systems may have an online version of the teaching application available on their website. If so, you may wish to download a copy of it to complete for your first draft, and then make the necessary corrections prior to its submission.

Dependent upon the particular school system, the completed application can be submitted in person, via U.S. mail, or online. If possible, submitting the application personally may afford you the opportunity to "put a face with your application." Introduce yourself to the secretarial (administrative) assistant, and if feasible, to a school administrator who will be involved in the application review process. This may provide an advantage in obtaining an interview.

Finally, maintain a copy of the completed teaching application for your files. Often school systems request similar types of information. Doing so allows you to take the information off one application and transfer it to another with minimal difficulty. And, as mentioned previously, after a sufficient period of time, call to confirm receipt of all application materials submitted.

The last component to address in the application and hiring process is managing your applications in an efficient and effective manner. Employing a systematic approach will assist greatly in keeping you organized during the job search process. One of the most efficient ways to do this is to create a "Prospective Teaching Position Contact Summary" table or worksheet. Refer to Figure 3 for a basic template. The table should include the following categories: (a) school system (district or county) and school name, (b) address

Figure 3. Prospective Teaching Positions Contact Summary Worksheet

School Contact Info	Cover Letter Sent	Resume Sent	Application Sent
Dr. John Smith Central City Public Schools Central City Middle School Central City, NC Phone: Fax:	4/26	4/26	4/26

and phone number of contact person, (c)letter of inquiry (cover letter) sent, (d)resume sent, (e)completed application sent, (f)credentials sent, (g)letters of recommendation requested, (h)letters of recommendation submitted, (i)interview scheduled, and (j)notes/comments. There may be additional categories you wish to develop above and beyond those recommended. Personalize the system as necessary to reflect your individual needs. Record dates in appropriate columns as tasks are completed; thereby providing an up-to-date table reflecting concise application-related data for your own reference in the midst of the job-hunt process.

In summary, there are several steps involved in the application and hiring process. The amount of time required to complete this process varies greatly from one school system to another. A general overview of the major steps involved from posting a teaching vacancy to hiring a teacher candidate for the position was provided. And, guidelines to employ when completing a teaching application, as well as a systematic means of tracking the status of each position applied for were identified.

Figure 3. (Continued)

Credentials Sent	Ref. Forms Requested	Ref. Forms Submitted	Interview Scheduled	Comments
5/10	4/24	5/2	5/20	VB coaching duty also

Teaching Portfolio as a Marketing Tool

A well-constructed teaching portfolio demonstrating your competencies as a teacher candidate can prove very beneficial in the application and hiring process. As a marketing tool, the teaching portfolio represents your "best works" to document selected abilities and competencies in the teaching profession. There are various types of content that may be appropriately included within the teaching portfolio (refer to Table 3). The following components are recommended to initiate portfolio development and construction: (a) resume, (b) statement of physical education teaching philosophy, (c) unit and lesson plans, (d) examples of teaching effectiveness, (e) assessment tools, (f) videotape of teaching, (g) photographs, (h) technology competencies, (i) extracurricular duties/activities, and (j) selected examples of student (preK-12) work (Ellery & Rauschenbach, 1997). Include examples/documents that best illustrate your teaching competencies and qualifications.

Table 3. Suggested Teaching Portfolio Contents*

- Resume
- Statement of Teaching Philosophy
- Unit and Lesson Plans
- Examples of Teaching Effectiveness
  - Systematic Observation Documentation
  - Video Analysis
  - Teaching Observations/Evaluations
- Assessment Tools Developed
  - Psychomotor, Cognitive, & Affective
  - Authentic
- Video Tape (Teaching "In Action")
- Photographs
- Technology Competencies
- Extracurricular Duties/Activities
- Examples of Student (PreK-12) Work

*Adapted from: Ellery, P., & Rauschenbach, J. (1997). Developing a professional portfolio. *Strategies, 11*(2), 10-12. Reston, VA: AAHPERD.

Each section of the portfolio should be clearly labeled so that the reader can locate specific types of information with ease. A table of contents and section dividers will assist to facilitate reader "maneuverability" as well. Plastic coversheets can be used to safeguard and protect portfolio documents. And, a three-ring binder (D-ring) with a clear cover insert on the front will serve as an appropriate "container" to house your portfolio documents. On the other hand, some teacher candidates may elect to develop electronic portfolios.

The teaching portfolio may be submitted in advance, during, or following a scheduled interview, dependent upon teacher candidate preference. Should you choose to do so in advance of an interview, submit the portfolio to the school administrator at least 2-3 days prior to the scheduled interview. This will allow sufficient time for the administrator to carefully review your portfolio documents at his or her convenience. In contrast, some teacher candidates choose to bring the teaching portfolio to the interview itself. Then, during the interview, candidates share their work in response to particular interview questions; thereby illustrating and clarifying designated teacher competencies and qualifications. Lastly, teacher candidates may elect to leave the portfolio with the administrator for review following the interview. Note that this provides ample time for an administrator to conduct a thorough review of the portfolio contents. There is not adequate time during the interview process itself to do justice in the attempt to conduct the portfolio review. If the portfolio is submitted for consideration following the interview, determine an agreed upon date for you to pick it up. Or, a teacher candidate can simply convey to school administrators that he/she has a portfolio available should the administrator wish to review it. The school administrator might then suggest when the portfolio review should occur.

Interview Strategies and Guidelines

Within this section, several components are addressed. First interview strategies and guidelines relative to pre-interview, interview, and post-interview aspects are discussed. Next, interview questions likely to be asked by school administrators are provided. Finally, questions that teacher candidates should ask during the interview process are also considered.

Pre-interview. Thus far, you succeeded in securing a job interview. It is critical to thoroughly prepare in advance to ensure a successful interview. First, investigate both the school and community context and surroundings. Find out as much as you can about the specific school system with which you are interviewing. Determine how physical education is viewed. How many days a week is physical education scheduled? What is the makeup of the student population? What is the socioeconomic status of the school and community? What school and community resources are available? How supportive are faculty and administrators of physical education? Are there other physical educators with whom you might be working should you accept the position? These are just some of the questions you may wish to inquire about as you prepare for the interview. You may acquire the answers to many of your questions just by spending some time on the school system's website. Picking up a local newspaper will provide insight on the local community as well. And, as you seek information, jot down questions that arise so that you may address them during the interview itself. The more you know about the school and community context, the greater the likelihood that a successful interview will be conducted.

Second, perform a "drive-through" in advance of the actual interview. Conduct a practice run of traveling to the interview location. Take into consideration any potential traveling nuances (traffic, railroad crossings, road construction, detours, etc.) that may impact the length of time required

Table 4. Administrator Interview Questions

- Tell me about yourself.
- Talk to me about your student teaching experience (units taught, levels, strengths, weaknesses, extracurricular duties, etc.).
- What are your hobbies/areas of interest?
- Of which 2-3 accomplishments are you most proud?
- What are 1-2 areas needing further development?
- What are the characteristics of an effective physical education teacher?
- How would you design a unit of instruction for this grade/activity?
- What types of activities do you feel are important to include in the physical education curriculum? Why?
- What instructional/teaching approaches do you employ?
- Describe your philosophy of teaching.
- How can you accommodate different learning styles? Skill levels?
- How might you assess student learning? What would be included in determining a student's physical education grade?
- What type of behavior management plan would you use in the development of a positive and productive learning environment?
- How would you handle a student who continually acted out in your class?
- How would you respond to the following scenario(s) [describe scenario(s)]?
- How might you communicate with parents?
- Describe today's student. What are the developmental characteristics of the student population?
- What motivation techniques would you employ for those students who don't like physical education?
- What experience do you have in working with diverse populations? How would you promote acceptance, tolerance, and diversity in your classes?
- How will you keep current in the field of physical education?
- Why do you want to teach at _____ School?
- What are your long-term professional goals?

Table 4. (continued)

- What do you have to offer with respect to enhancing our current physical education program?
- What types of extracurricular duties are you willing to assume?
- Describe, from bell to bell, a typical lesson in your class.
- What types of fitness assessments would you recommend using and why?
- How would you motivate a student who continually does not dress for class and/or participate?
- How do you feel about using exercise as a discipline technique?
- Are you involved professionally in your state or national organization?

to get to the designated interview site. Determine the actual travel time and add additional time to ensure that you arrive for the interview in a timely fashion (5 to 10 minutes ahead of scheduled interview appointment).

Third, develop responses to "practice interview questions." Refer to Table 4, Administrator Interview Questions, to use in preparation. If possible, search out an individual you know to conduct a "mock" interview (Rikard & Senne, 1996). Rehearsing for the interview will allow you to field and respond to questions in advance, rather than going into the interview blind.

Finally, thoroughly review your copy of the completed teaching application submitted in response to the job vacancy. Most administrators will use it in formulation of some of their interview questions. Addressing all strategies and guidelines provided above in advance of the interview will improve the likelihood of a successful interview.

Interview. Several strategies and guidelines are applicable during the actual interview itself. First, consider professional attire and grooming aspects. Conservative dress and appearance are strongly recommended. Grooming should be conservative as well. Second, follow proper social etiquette or general courtesies. Arrive shortly before the scheduled interview appointment and introduce yourself to the receptionist as you enter the interview location. When introducing yourself, or being introduced to another individual, offer a firm handshake. This will often be regarded as a sign of confidence.

Third, be prepared and well organized. Carry some type of professional folder, brief case, or binder to secure the materials you've brought with you for reference. A writing pad, ink pen, and sufficient paper are also needed, so that you may take notes during the interview. Additionally, you may wish to bring a few extra copies of your resume, as well as a list of references if not provided in the resume itself.

Fourth, convey confidence throughout the interview process via appropriate body and verbal language. Smile and use direct eye contact with the interviewer(s). Avoid using nervous mannerisms (hands in pocket, hands rattling papers, biting nails), as well as distracting verbal mannerisms ("and um," "uh huh"). These gestures tend to shift the focus away from what you are attempting to convey; thereby, drawing attention to the specific mannerism displayed.

Fifth, when responding to questions posed by the interviewer, take a few seconds to "gather your thoughts" prior to initiating your response. Furthermore, elaborate on your response by providing appropriate examples to clarify. Effective communications skills are critical. Speak clearly and concisely. Market yourself, but do appear to be overconfident in your abilities. Know going into the interview what extracurricular duties you are qualified to assume, in addition to the normal teaching duties. Do not overextend or overcommit yourself. Effective planning and preparation during the first few years of teaching requires a great deal of time. Often administrators seek out novice teachers because they feel that they can get them to commit to several activities above and beyond their contracted teaching responsibilities. In actuality, the "experienced" teachers should be the ones to assume more after-school related activities, since they've had sufficient time and experience to develop, create, and implement their instructional responsibilities. Carefully consider what you are willing to take on in addition to your designated teaching responsibilities. Furthermore, you might inquire as to what extracurricular activities are included in the job description, and allow that to be a factor to consider and/or negotiate should the job offer actually be extended.

Finally, the typical interviewer/school administrator will ask his or her set of questions relative to the position for which you are interviewing. In general, he or she will begin the interview with some "warm-up" or "ice-breaker" questions to assist in putting you at ease. Then, he or she will proceed to the heart of the interview, asking questions relative to the teaching, behavioral, managerial, and instructional aspects. Afterward, you will have an opportunity to ask questions concerning the teaching position. At the closure of the interview, it is recommended that you inquire as to the anticipated time frame for making the hiring decision. This will at least provide you with an approximate date by which the position will be filled, and will be beneficial to you in scheduling additional interviews, or making a decision regarding a teaching offer. Finally, close the interview with another firm handshake and thank the administrator for the opportunity to interview as you depart. If you are still interested in the position at the close of the interview, be certain to convey this sentiment to the administrator. Remember, both you and the administrator are attempting to determine how good the match is with respect to the teaching position.

Post-interview. Following the interview, it is recommended that the teacher candidate send a short thank-you letter to the school administrator with whom he or she interviewed. Secondly, wait patiently to hear from the school system. Although it may be three or four weeks since the interview, this does not necessarily imply that you didn't get the job. There could be numerous reasons as to why you've not been contacted thus far. Refer to the allotted hiring decision time frame. If it is still within the time frame designated by the school system, do not harass them by calling or e-mailing them several times a week. Rather, continue to submit teaching applications for appropriate positions. It is never a good idea to assume that you will automatically be hired for the position. It is important to remain optimistic, yet you must be realistic as well.

Administrator interview questions. Table 4 provides a list of potential questions that may be posed by school administrators as they interview candidates for teaching vacancies. These questions were derived from a variety of resources that may be accessed in Table 6., Available Resources. Develop responses to each of the sample questions provided in preparation for the interview. Also, be familiar with social, psychological, physiological, cognitive, and psychomotor characteristics of students, and how these characteristics might impact learning and instruction. Similarly, diversity is a hot topic that you must be prepared to address as well. Finally, it is also important to become familiar with the state curriculum guide for physical education, in addition to NASPE Standards for K-12 Physical Education.

Teacher candidate interview questions. During the interview, the teacher candidate will also be offered opportunities to ask questions. Table 5 supplies a list of potential questions that may be asked by the teacher candidate during the interview process. Additional questions may be accessed from resources provided in Table 6., Available Resources. In addition, you may wish to talk with some of the current faculty if feasible. Request to view both the facilities (indoor and outdoor) and the physical education equipment. Do your best to get a strong indication as to whether administration and faculty are supportive of physical education as a part of the school curriculum. Keep in mind that you are trying to determine how well suited you are for the teaching position, and whether the match is a good one.

Table 5. Teacher Candidate Interview Questions

- What is _____ School's mission/vision?
- What is the teacher/student ratio in physical education classes?
- What incentives are provided to encourage teachers to earn advanced degrees? Professional development opportunities?
- Do teachers participate in the curriculum review process? In what ways?
- What support staff is available to assist teachers?
- What specific discipline procedures does _____ School enforce?
- What types of inservice/mentoring programs are provided to beginning teachers?
- Are the parents/community supportive of the school? Of physical education?
- Are school administrators/faculty supportive of physical education?
- What allowances are provided for teacher supplies, equipment, and materials?
- How much money is allocated for the physical education budget, and who determines the requisitions?
- How are teachers assigned to extracurricular activities? Is compensation provided?
- What additional duties (above and beyond the classroom) must all teachers assume? (i.e., homeroom, bus duty).
- What are the prospects for future growth in the community? Schools?
- What type of administration/management style is employed at the school?
- Can I view equipment and facilities used for physical education instruction?
- Can I talk with current physical education teachers or other school faculty/personnel?
- What is the time frame in making a decision to fill this teaching position?

Job Search Techniques

Gaining access to information concerning available teaching positions can be handled in a variety of ways. However, your college/university's career services office should be your first contact in the job search process. They have many available resources and professionally trained personnel to assist in all aspects of the job search process including: (a) setting up a teaching credentials file, (b) developing cover letters and resume, (c) listing of job fairs, (d) sponsoring on-campus career days, (e) polishing interview skills, (f) keeping job postings and applications, (g) providing free publications to assist in the job search process, and (h) offering career counseling. Career services is a good place to begin, and might open the door to a number of viable options to assist you in the job search.

Networking is another job search option worth pursuing. If you are considering staying in the vicinity of where you've attended college, you may wish to start networking via your student teaching internship site. Often, teachers within the school systems are first to know about potential or available teaching vacancies, long before the actual teaching position is advertised. As such, networking with teachers can become one of your best options.

Alternatively, networking among college professors and the school of education or director of clinical experiences at your college/university can be constructive in the job search process as well. Frequently, methods professors who direct teaching practicum experiences (field experiences) within the public school system are informed of upcoming teaching vacancies. And, many school systems within proximity to the college/university will invariably call the school of education or clinical experiences office to inquire as to potential candidates that may be a good match for their particular teaching vacancy. In addition, most schools of education generally have an accessible bulletin board where available teaching positions are posted. These are generally updated on a regular basis, so check them periodically for new postings.

Several states conduct regular teaching job fairs in conjunction with county and school district systems. Teacher candidates can visit a large number of potential school systems in a single day by attending a job fair. Should you choose to pursue this route, dress professionally and bring a large number of resumes for distribution to potential school systems. Often, school systems will also be setup to conduct onsite interviews, and some will even choose to hire on the spot. Consequently, this job search tactic can be quite advantageous, and is strongly recommended as an option to pursue.

Additionally, the Sunday classifieds sections in local and major metropolitan newspapers provide another source to investigate in the search for a teaching position. Usually the teacher candidate is limited with this option, since most listed teaching positions will be local. Typically, teacher candidates will need to couple this particular tactic with other search techniques as well to familiarize themselves with a larger pool of potential vacancies.

In contrast, the Internet can be one of the best and most efficient resources to use in the search for available teaching positions. Teacher candidates are able to cover a lot of territory in a short amount of time by taking advantage of this option. First, there are national websites available, such as USteach and Dantes' Troops to Teachers that serve as large databases for teaching positions in every subject area across most of the United States. The URLs for these websites can be found in in Table 6., Available Resources. These websites are particularly valuable to those who are interested in teaching in another state. Another tactic that can be used via the Internet entails visiting the web pages of state departments of education, county/ district school systems, and individual schools as well. Most of these websites will have a link to a teacher employment web page from which to access available teaching vacancy postings. In addition, teacher candidates may be able to access information regarding upcoming teacher job fairs from these sites as well. Some states, such as South Carolina, even offer teaching applications and reference forms that can be completed and submitted online.

Available Resources

Table 6 contains a select number of resources available to teacher candidates as they begin the job-hunt process. Resources are organized by the following categories: (a) general publications, (b) job search Internet sites, (c) interview info, (d) NASPE publications, and (e) portfolios. Although limited in number and narrow in focus, the resources provided are extremely valuable to teacher candidates in pursuit of their first teaching position.

Table 6. Available Resources

General Publications:
- *2001 Job Search Handbook for Educators*, American Association for Employment in Education, 820 Davis St., Suite 222, Evanston, IL, 60201-4445. Phone: (847) 864-1999.
- *Career Development Guide* (1999-2000). CASS Recruitment Media: http://www.placementmanual.com

Internet Job Search Sites:
- Dantes' Troops to Teachers: http://www.jobs2teach.doded.mil/
- National Center for Careers in Education: http://www.usteach.com

Interview Information:
- Clement, M. (September 2002). Help wanted: How to hire the best teachers. *Principal Leadership, 3*(1), 16-21.
- Lavington, C. *A polished interview.* (pamphlet). Douglassville, PA: Kiwi Brands, Inc.
- NASPE. *Suggested job interview questions for prospective physical education teachers.* www.naspeinfo.org (Issues & Action, Position Papers)
- Rikard, G., & Senne, T. (1996). A mock interview: Preservice teachers and principals interact. *JOPERD, 67*(3), 16-17. Reston, VA: AAHPERD.

Table 6. (continued)

NASPE Publications:

- Mohnsen, B. (Ed.). (2003). *Concepts and principles of physical education: What every student needs to know* (2nd ed.). Reston, VA: NASPE.
- NASPE. (1995). *Appropriate practices for middle school physical education.* Reston, VA: Author.
- NASPE. (1998). *Appropriate practices for high school physical education.* Reston, VA: Author.
- NASPE. (2000). *Appropriate practices for elementary school physical education.* Reston, VA: Author.
- NASPE. (2004a). *Moving into the future: National physical education standards.* Reston, VA: Author.
- NASPE. (2004b). *Physical activity for children: A statement of guidelines for children ages 5-12 (2nd ed.).* Reston, VA: Author.
- NASPE Assessment Series for K-12 Physical Education and Professional Preparation (multiple publications). Reston, VA: Author.

Portfolios:

- Ellery, P., & Rauschenbach, J. (1997). Developing a professional portfolio. *Strategies, 11*(2), 10-12. Reston, VA: AAHPERD.
- Lumpkin, A. (1996). Professional practice: Develop a portfolio: Hone your teaching skills. *Strategies, 10*(1), 15-17. Reston, VA: AAHPERD.
- Melograno, V. (1998). *Professional and student portfolios for physical education.* Champaign, IL: Human Kinetics.
- Melograno, V. (2000). *Preservice professional portfolio system.* Reston, VA: AAHPERD Publications.

PART II - Get Set...

There are several core aspects of teaching that can be addressed once you've signed a teaching contract. Developing the physical education curriculum,
instructional units, classroom management plan, assessment and grading system, and a record-keeping scheme can be done, at least in part, prior to the start of the school year. Effective use of this time will be well spent in helping to get the new school year off to a good start.

Since most physical education teacher education (PETE) programs address curriculum development, instructional planning, and assessment in great detail, they are not covered within the scope of this text. However, curriculum development, instructional planning, and assessment are key components to preparing for the start of your new school year; therefore, beginning teachers will dedicate much time to these. As part of preparation for the start of the school year, Part II will focus specifically on aspects of developing and implementing a classroom management plan and record-keeping schemes.

Chapter 2   Developing a Classroom Management Plan
Chapter 3   Record Keeping

Classroom Rules

1. 1. Always be prepared for class.
(This addresses appropriate dress for
participation, assignment, etc.)
2. Safety is our number one priority. (This rule
refers to spatial awareness, appropriate use of
equipment, adherence to rules, etc.)
3. Show respect for others and the learning
environment. (Topics could include respect for
teacher, peers, equipment, etc.)
4. Put forth your best effort always. (Students
who put for good efforts stay on task, work
hard, etc.)
5. Encourage and support one another in all
learning activities. (Students adhere to this rule
by showing cooperation, encouragement,
positive affective behaviors, sports conduct, etc.)

Chapter 2
Developing a Classroom Management Plan

Much thought and preparation on classroom management should occur prior to the start of the school year. Failure to do so can almost guarantee at least challenging, if not devastating, results for a beginning teacher. Creating an appropriate and productive learning environment is critical to achieving success in teaching and student learning. Consequently, the following management elements should be considered: (a) school policies, (b) rules, (c) protocols/procedures, (d) consequences, (e) preventive behavior management, (f) behavior management models and strategies, (g) motivation techniques, and (h) implementation.

The following recommendations must be modified appropriately to address the specific context of your school and the corresponding grade levels you teach. Use these as a guide and select from those most appropriately aligned with your own personal management style and school context. Note that you may need to conform to an existing classroom management plan. In that case, you may be able to gradually provide input and negotiate some aspects of the plan currently in existence.

School Policies

Upon hiring, request a copy of the school's policy handbook if not initially provided one. A school policy handbook outlines all policies and procedures to be followed by teachers (i.e., attendance; excused/unexcused absences; fire, tornado, and other-related emergency procedures; student injury; discipline protocol) during the course of the school year. In addition, some schools also issue a student/parent handbook as well as a faculty handbook. Beginning teachers should carefully review and acquaint themselves with these documents to prepare a classroom management plan. Then, once a draft of the classroom management plan has been developed, it's a good idea to verify its alignment with all school policies and procedures.

Rules

Physical education rules specify those behaviors students need to avoid or exhibit in order to provide an appropriate learning environment for all students (Siedentop & Tannehill, 2000). There are several guidelines that will assist teachers in the development of an effective set of classroom rules. First, rules should be short and direct, while being conveyed in an age-appropriate manner. It is best to only have a few rules; four to seven is a general rule of thumb. Incorporating more-encompassing rules allows for addressing a multitude of mini rules. For example, the rule "try hard" can include behaviors such as using time well, staying on task, and putting forth an effort to learn. Siedentop and Tannehill (2000) also suggest some overriding categories for developing physical education rules: (a)safety, (b)respect for others, (c)respect for the learning environment, (d)support the learning of others, and (e)try hard. Each of these categories should be explicitly addressed in rules development.

A potential set of physical education rules might include:

1. Always be prepared for class. (This addresses appropriate dress for participation, assignments, etc.)
2. Safety is our number one priority. (This rule refers to spatial awareness, appropriate use of equipment, adherence to rules, etc.)
3. Show respect for others and the learning environment. (Topics could include respect for teacher, peers, equipment, etc.)
4. Put forth your best effort always. (Students who put for good efforts stay on task, work hard, etc.)
5. Encourage and support one another in all learning activities. (Students adhere to this rule by showing cooperation, encouragement, positive affective behaviors, sports conduct, etc.)

The rules above are geared toward middle or high school students. How could they be revised to appropriately address elementary school students in physical education?

Furthermore, rules should be stated positively; however, both positive and negative examples should be provided for clarification. And finally, at the beginning of the school year, teachers need to prompt students to follow rules often; provide frequent, specific feedback; and consistently offer positive reinforcement to students in compliance.

Protocols/Procedures

In contrast to rules, protocols or procedures are *routines* that occur on a regular basis in physical education class, including all procedural aspects of lessons that recur on a frequent basis. Siedentop and Tannehill (2000) provide 12 typical physical education protocol categories: (a)entry, (b)attention/quiet, (c)home base, (d)gather, (e)disperse, (f)gain attention,

(g) retrieve, (h) partners, (i) finish, (j) leave, (k) boundaries, and (l) housekeeping. Beginning teachers should select protocol categories appropriate to the school context and grade levels to be taught. For example, showering (which falls into the housekeeping category) would not apply to elementary school students. However, the home base and gather categories can easily apply to both elementary and secondary level programs.

Entry refers to how and what students are to do upon entering the gym. *Attention/quiet* denotes the teacher's signal and students' response to the same. *Home base* might represent an overall organizational format used, such as squads or teams. *Gather* specifies a method by which students move from a dispersed to a central location, as well as how to organize at that location. *Gain attention* is the means by which students appropriately request the teacher's attention. *Retrieve* indicates procedures by which students regain possession of a ball/equipment when it has left their designated practice area. The term *partners* refers to specific relationship organizational patterns including trios, quads, and so forth. *Finish* denotes routines for cool-down and closure components of the lesson. *Leave* indicates the pattern used to leave classroom space and return to the locker room or go to the next class. *Boundaries* specify designated "working" space during the lesson. Finally, *housekeeping* denotes all procedural aspects relative to dressing, jewelry, bathroom use, drinks, and related aspects.

Developing protocols or procedures for the categories above provides the novice teacher with a fairly comprehensive set of physical education protocols. Once developed, some key recommendations for actual implementation are in order. First, when feasible, teachers should incorporate student input in developing class rules. The rationale for this is as follows: If students are involved in the process, they are more likely to become vested, and thereby, "buy in" to the rules established.

Second, a teacher may need to develop special rules or protocols during certain types of content or circumstances. For example, if you teach a gymnastics unit, you will have rules (i.e., spotting, apparatus, use of space) specific to the particular unit content, in addition to standard physical education rules. Third, protocols need to be taught as specifically as one would teach motor skills. Let me share an example to illustrate this point. After four years of teaching high school physical education, I accepted a job as a middle school physical education teacher, grades 6-8. I was greeted with a rude awakening the first day sixth-grade girls were going to dress in physical education uniforms. Note that prior to this point in time, the only changing that occurred in physical education was changing into gym shoes.

I became quite frustrated. You see, we spent more time in the locker room that first day than we did in the gym. Since this was their first experience with locker rooms and changing clothes for class, there were many aspects I *assumed* female students would know and be able to do without instruction on my part. Instead, much time was spent during the next several days, getting a handle on locker room procedures prior to starting the class on time in an effective manner. The girls needed to be taught several procedures: (a) how to open a lock, (b) where to put the lock when changing so that someone else didn't mistake it for hers, (c) getting in and out of the shower, (d) distributing and collecting towels, and so on. In subsequent years, I planned well for these locker room protocols by teaching specific locker room routines for the girls to follow prior to entering the gym for class. By doing so, routines were established in a timely manner, thus making for both a happier teacher, and well adapted students to the locker-room experience.

Consequently, rehearsing protocol or routines, as described above, will help students learn the specific steps that you wish to occur as they embark upon a particular procedure. Although it may take time before these routines are polished, it is important to reward student progress toward established expectations. Frequent teacher feedback and encouragement, checks for student understanding, along with the use of learning activities to teach and practice set protocols will lead to a well-developed, efficient, and productive learning environment for both teacher and students alike. In sum, established protocols should reduce management time; allowing for efficient organization, allocation, and management of time, space, and activities in a manner conducive to learning.

Consequences

In tandem with physical education rules, consequences for violations of the same must be put in place. This is commonly referred to as the discipline component of behavior management. While some school systems employ whole-school behavior management plans, most often there is a level of flexibility for individual teachers to develop consequences suited to their particular style and needs. Again, prior to developing a set of consequences for inappropriate behavior, it is important to review any school policies that may apply.

The primary goal of initiating consequences is to stop the misbehavior immediately. This is the short-term solution to the problem. More long-term intervention strategies will also need to be employed to realize an acceptable change in student behavior over time. A teacher should establish *levels of consequences* appropriate to the developmental level of the students. Levels of consequences provide for sequential and more-rigorous penalties, progressing from less to more severe, depending on the particular misbehavior or repeated misbehaviors exhibited. Several levels of consequences should be established. A first-level consequence (minor infraction, least severe) might consist of a verbal warning. A second-level consequence might be an abbreviated time out. An extended time out could serve as a third-level consequence. Examples of fourth-level consequences might include a parent phone call or a detention. Subsequently, a fifth-level consequence (most severe) could entail a referral to the principal. The examples provided are merely that—examples. As a teacher, it will be critical for you to determine what types of consequences align with your personal behavior management philosophy, and most appropriately address the needs of your students, in order to create a productive learning environment for all students. The key to developing an effective set of consequences is to determine actions that will discourage misbehavior, while encouraging appropriate behavior.

One elementary physical education program with which I am familiar employs what they call a "three-strike policy." Strike one is a verbal warning, where inappropriate behavior is brought to the attention of the designated offender. Oftentimes, he or she is also gently reminded of what would be considered appropriate behavior. Strike two signals a short time out for the individual student; whereby he or she must then apologize for the inappropriate behavior and indicate the appropriate way to behave. Once done, the student can rejoin the class. Finally, if strike three is called on an individual student, he or she is "out" for the remainder of the class. Subsequently, a phone call or letter will go home to parents/guardians that must be signed and returned during the next class. Sometimes, students must also complete a sheet indicating the inappropriate behavior as well as what he or she needs to do in order to behave appropriately.

One consequence that should never be employed by a physical education teacher is the use of exercise as punishment/consequence. This is absolutely inappropriate, and its inappropriateness is substantiated in several NASPE position statements. Does it work to stop inappropriate behavior? Yes, for the short term, but the long-term damage can be irreparable. One of our goals as physical educators is to get students to enjoy physical activity in hopes that they will continue to be physically active throughout their lifetimes. Using exercise as a form of punishment negates this goal.

Anecdotally, I have taught numerous physical education courses for elementary education majors. I always began the course by having students write about their K-12 physical education experiences. Most were very negative, and "exercise as punishment" was revealed as a prime indicator for their dislike of physical education.

The consequences you develop will be based on the behavior management or discipline model you select to serve as the conceptual framework for the types of actions you choose to employ to deter inappropriate behavior. Refer to the subsequent section on behavior management models and strategies for insight into developing appropriate and effective consequences for student misbehavior.

Preventive Behavior Management

The key to effective behavior management is to reduce the number of opportunities for inappropriate behavior to occur. A key problem for beginning teachers is time management. If teachers have not carefully planned for and organized transitions that will occur during the physical education lesson, down time will occur. Consequently, the likelihood of opportunities for inappropriate behavior to occur increases during down time. Thus, one preventive behavior management strategy is to *reduce down time* through careful planning of managerial and organizational aspects of the lesson (i.e., use of time, space, equipment, transitions from one activity to the next). Organizational patterns can also be used to separate problem students so they are grouped primarily with students who behave appropriately, rather than allowing the opportunity for problem students to position themselves within the same group.

Creating developmentally motivating and challenging physical education lessons provides a second preventive behavior management strategy. Developmentally appropriate lessons will ensure that all students are working at a level that allows for approximately an 80% success rate in terms of practice opportunities (Graham, Holt/Hale, & Parker, 2001). Employing upward and downward extensions (Rink, 2002) can help achieve this goal. Gear the learning tasks to the skill level of the majority of the class. Then, determine how the task can be made simpler (downward extension) or more complex (upward extension). Tasks can be varied by modifying equipment used, amount of space, speed, pathways, force, number of students, etc. Students unable to achieve the 80% target success rate (or whatever level you've established as target) can then move to a downward extension, while those that attain a greater than 80% success rate can transition to a more challenging and complex learning task (upward extension). Extensions (upward and downward) can assist in keeping students on task. Oftentimes, if students are unsuccessful or unchallenged with the planned learning tasks, they tend to get off task or bored, generally leading to inappropriate behavior.

Tasks must be motivating as well as challenging. Beginning teachers can provide for motivating lessons by *using application tasks* (Rink, 2002) as part of their content development repertoire. Self-testing activities and modified games employing skills developed during the lesson can help keep students motivated. *Goal-setting* is another avenue that can be pursued. Students can challenge themselves to attain a certain level of competency. The use of a goal in learning tasks serves as a means to maintain student focus on the task at hand, subsequently leading to more on-task than off-task behavior.

Additionally, beginning teachers can structure learning tasks to resemble how the skills are employed in the game context. This can be done once students are able to perform designated skills in isolation with control. Subsequently, skills can be combined in game-like contexts so students practice the skills in the manner in which they will occur in the game, whether it be a low-organized, modified, or sport-specific game. For example at the secondary level, when students exhibit competency in performing the volleyball forearm pass in isolation, demonstrating control of both self and the equipment, the teacher might progress to performing the forearm pass from the back row to the middle front position from a ball tossed to the hitter, first from his or her own side of the net, and then from the opposite side of the net. A goal of correctly passing three out of five tosses to the middle front position, so the ball is settable, can then be used as an application task. Ideally, the goal will continue to motivate students during the lesson, leading to an increased likelihood of on-task behavior. Likewise, this same principle can be employed with skill themes and movement concepts. Once a student has learned to perform a ground kick using the correct technique to send the ball to a stationary target, he or she may then work to combine it with dribbling in various pathways in general space, and then taking a shot on goal, hitting the target no fewer than three out of five attempts.

Using a variety of teaching approaches can also lead to fewer behavior management problems. Initially, beginning teachers will employ direct instruction. This is appropriate as they first begin a teaching position. However, once they become familiar with their students, their capabilities and preferences, beginning teachers should begin to vary their instructional or teaching approaches. They will need to consider numerous factors in determining which approaches will work best within the designated context (Metzler, 2000). Inquiry, tactical games, cooperative learning, personalized system for instruction, sport education, and peer teaching represent several instructional models or teaching approaches that can be employed, which provide a spectrum of teacher-directed and student-directed choices.

Keeping students actively engaged during a physical education lesson will further help to prevent behavior management problems. This can be accomplished by providing students with maximum practice opportunities. Down time is produced if students have to wait their turn to gain practice attempts; hence, they have opportunities for misbehavior. Organizing so that wait time is nonexistent or at least limited, and providing for a sufficient amount of equipment will help allow more students practice opportunities.

Furthermore, the use of *scanning* and/or *withitness*, as well as *appropriate teacher positioning* can be employed as preventive behavior management strategies. Scanning the class in a systematic manner will help beginning teachers stay on top of things. They will know where students are located and what specifically they are doing. This is critical, especially in new teaching positions. Similarly, learning student names as soon as possible will assist in the beginning teacher's management of the classroom. Once teachers get to know their students, they can quickly scan those that tend to cause problems to make sure they are participating in an appropriate manner. A teacher is said to have withitness when he or she knows what's going on in the class at all times. Often these teachers are depicted as having "eyes in the back of their heads," since they are always "in the know" about what's happening at any given point in time during the class period. This particular skill takes practice and will become further developed with experience. Back-to-the-wall or perimeter teacher positioning will assist in the employment of both scanning and withitness techniques.

One technique that will help beginning teachers gain an extra pair of eyes is the use of cross-group feedback (Ryan & Yerg, 2001). Providing feedback to students who are positioned on the other side of the gym sends a message indicating that although the teacher is a distance away, he or she is watching and monitoring. Additionally, teacher positioning can also play a critical role in preventive behavior management. Teacher movement patterns during the lesson should be unpredictable, while providing a clear view of all students. A typical mistake made by beginning teachers is to position themselves directly in front of the class throughout the lesson. Generally speaking, students who are likely to behave inappropriately will position themselves as far away from the teacher as possible, hoping to elude consequences that might follow. If the teacher employs unpredictable movement patterns throughout the lesson, the opportunity for misbehavior decreases.

A final recommendation in preventive behavior management is to *positively reinforce and/or reward appropriate behavior.* Beginning teachers have a tendency to bring attention to inappropriate rather than appropriate student behavior. This provides attention to the misbehaving student, while providing no reinforcement or recognition for students choosing to behave appropriately. Often, appropriate behavior will increase if it is recognized and positively reinforced or rewarded by the teacher. This is an excellent strategy for beginning teachers to employ as they attempt to prevent behavior problems from occurring in the classroom. Refer to the *Motivation Techniques* section for selected examples.

In summary, several preventive behavior management strategies have been described. While many more exist, the strategies provided can serve as a foundation upon which beginning physical education teachers can build as they work to create a productive learning environment for all students.

Behavior Management Models and Strategies

There are numerous behavior management models that have been developed over the last several decades. Teachers can choose various discipline/behavior management strategies existing within each model that will effectively dovetail with their personal management styles. The key to initiating the development an effective behavior management model is to reflectively consider your own philosophy (beliefs and assumptions) concerning behavior management. A teacher's behavior management philosophy should form the basis of his or her discipline or behavior management model, along with subsequent strategies or techniques employed. For example, if a teacher believes that all students who misbehave in a certain context should receive the same consequence, then it will be important for him or her to select a model that aligns with this belief.

It is beyond the scope of this text to provide an extensive compendium of models and strategies; therefore, beginning teachers should seek information on selected behavior management/discipline models by conducting library and/or electronic searches on models of interest. After developing a philosophy of behavior management, explore and investigate models to determine a "best fit" for your behavior management model. It may be that you are attracted to features from a variety of models. If so, take the most compelling features of each to design your own system of discipline/behavior management. Keep in mind that you will also need to consider any existing management plan currently in place (if there is one). It is wise go into a teaching position knowing what you'd like to do in terms of behavior management; however, you may need to compromise and or negotiate this initially if a fairly effective system is already in place.

A separate, personal, and social responsibility model, *Teaching Personal and Social Responsibility* (TPSR), was initially developed by Hellison (1978) in the physical education context. As designed, TPSR is considered an *instructional*, rather than a *behavioral* model. And, although not developed intentionally as a behavior management model, its goals and levels of responsibility are readily employed by physical education practitioners throughout the United States in some form or another as part of their behavior management system. It is based on the following premise: "...responsibility encompasses both *learning to become more responsible* and *learning to take responsibility* within the context of physical education instruction and its transfer outside the gym" (Hellison, 1996, p. 271). "TPSR offers a specific set of goals (or levels)

Table 7. Teaching Personal and Social Responsibility (TSPR) Goals*

I. Respect for the rights and feeling of others
   a. Maintaining self-control
   b. Respecting everyone's right to be included
   c. Respecting everyone's right to a peaceful conflict resolution
II. Participation and effort
   a. Exploring effort
   b. Trying new things
   c. Developing a personal definition of success
III. Self-Direction
   a. Demonstrating on-task independence
   b. Developing a sound knowledge base
   c. Developing, carrying out, and evaluating a personal plan
   d. Balancing current and future needs
   e. "Striving against external forces" (deCharms, 1976)
IV. Sensitivity and responsiveness to the well-being of others
   a. Developing prerequisite interpersonal skills
   b. Becoming sensitive and compassionate
   c. Contributing to the community and beyond
   d. Helping others without rewards
V. Outside the gym
   a. Trying out the levels in the classroom, on the playground and street, and at home
   b. Making decisions about the usefulness of the levels outside the gym

*Reprinted, by permission, from D. Hellison. (2003). Teaching personal and social responsibility in physical education. In S. J. Silverman & C. D. Ennis (Eds.), *Student learning in physical education* (2nd ed., p. 244). Champaign, IL: Human Kinetics.

Table 8. Cumulative Levels of Responsibility*

Level 0—Irresponsibility: Students who operate at Level 0 make excuses and blame others for their behavior and deny personal responsibility for what they do or fail to do.

Level I—Respect: Students at Level I may not participate in the day's activities or show much mastery or improvement, but they are able to control their behavior enough so that they don't interfere with other students' right to learn or the teacher's right to teach. And they do this without being prompted by the teacher very much and without constant supervision.

Level II—Participation: Students at Level II not only show minimal respect to others but also participate in the subject matter. They willingly, even enthusiastically play, accept challenges, practice motor skills, and train for fitness under the teacher's supervision.

Level III—Self-Direction: Students at Level III not only show respect and participation, but they are also able to work without direct supervision. They can identify their own needs and can begin to plan and execute their own physical education programs.

Level IV—Caring: Students at Level IV, in addition to respecting others, participating, and being self-directed, are motivated to extend their sense of responsibility beyond themselves by cooperating, giving support, showing concern, and helping.

*Reprinted, by permission, from D. Hellison. (2003). Teaching personal and social responsibility in physical education. In S. J. Silverman & C. D. Ennis (Eds.), *Student learning in physical education* (2nd ed., p. 245). Champaign, IL: Human Kinetics.

and strategies for teaching kids to take more responsibility for their own well-being and their relationships with others" (Hellison, 1996, p. 282). The model identifies five goals as guidelines for becoming more responsible. The goals are presented as a hierarchy of sorts, implying that one must meet previous level qualifications prior to progressing toward achievement of a higher level of responsibility. Hellison further developed these goals into levels of responsibility. In doing so, he provided an avenue by which teachers and students could discuss progress toward higher levels of responsibility. The TPSR goals and cumulative levels of responsibility are outlined in Tables 7 and 8 (Hellison, 2003). Hellison's TPSR model provides a framework from which to work toward development of responsible and caring students in the context of physical education. This model has been employed at all program levels (elementary, middle, and high school); and therefore, can serve as a critical component of a beginning physical educator's comprehensive plan for behavior management and creating a productive learning environment for all students.

Motivation Techniques

Motivation techniques are the means and incentives by which physical educators are able to motivate their students to promote a productive and effective learning environment. Effective motivation techniques will facilitate appropriate student behavior, while reducing inappropriate behavior. Motivation techniques should include both intrinsic and extrinsic forms of incentives. Additionally, physical education teachers should provide individual as well as whole-class incentives to assist in the production of an effective learning environment. It will be important to keep the developmental level of your students in mind as you design and create incentives for your classroom. And, as a new teacher, you are only limited by your imagination in the development of motivation techniques.

Positive reinforcement can be employed as an individual and/or whole-class motivation technique. It can be conveyed through verbal and nonverbal teacher actions. "Way to go," "I like the way Jake's squad is organized and ready to go," and "Nice job of working with Meaghan on her serve" provide a few examples of positive verbal reinforcement. In contrast, a teacher can also use positive nonverbal reinforcement by giving students "high fives" or "thumbs up," etc. Each of these positive reinforcement techniques conveys recognition for appropriate behavior and acceptance. Beginning teachers will need to use discretion in determining whether it's best to convey the positive reinforcement one-on-one, or to offer recognition in front of peers, based upon the individual student and context.

"Student of the Day" is another motivation technique used by many physical educators. In this scenario, one student from each physical education class is selected at the end of the period as the student of the day. Typically, this student has exhibited exceptional behavior, good sports conduct, and other types of appropriate behaviors. Usually, he or she is given a certificate for this honor and is recognized by the rest of the class. A wise physical education teacher will keep track of these awards, ensuring that all students in the class at one time or another receive this award.

A *"Take 10"* award could be used to motivate groups of students within a class (squads, teams, etc.) or the entire class to behave in a manner conducive to learning. If a group or class was deemed the winner of the behavioral competition (based on points accumulated for exemplary behavior), they would be given the opportunity to select a physical activity of their own choosing for the last 10 minutes of class. Needless to say, this type of award would not be appropriate to use on a daily basis, but now and again, it might offer good incentive for complying with, and going above and beyond, teacher expectations.

Sometimes peer pressure can be used in an effort to get students to act appropriately. A *whole-class reward system* could be put into place. The goal would be for the class to earn x amount of points (or tokens) for displaying behavior appropriate for a productive learning environment, and would encompass a range of appropriate affective behaviors. A record-keeping system could be put in place to track class progress toward the established goal. Inappropriate student behavior could result in a deduction of points or tokens from those previously acquired for good behavior. Students would encourage appropriate behavior in their peers in order to earn the rewards. The teacher could provide a selection of different rewards from which to choose.

Oftentimes, students misbehave to gain the attention of both teacher and students. A teacher might find it beneficial to put this type of student in a *leadership role* (leading warm-ups, handing out equipment) as a motivating technique. This can be constructive in that it replaces the misbehavior with a role whereby the student can acquire the attention he or she needs without disrupting the class. Both teacher and student can win in this context.

One middle school motivation technique that was used to encourage appropriate behavior throughout the entire school also comes to mind. Teachers were given *"I caught you being good!" slips.* Each teacher was given a designated number of slips that they could hand out to deserving students at any time. While sometimes the slips would be issued to students in the respective teacher's class, often they were awarded to students during lunch, homeroom, and in the halls at various points throughout the day. Once again, this provided another means of recognizing students that behaved appropriately, and, although the example was derived from a middle school practice, it could easily be employed at the elementary school level as well.

A variation of "I caught you being good" is sending a letter home to parents or guardians. It could be typed as a form letter with space provided to write in the good actions of the particular student. Most parents receive letters from teachers for inappropriate behavior displayed by their children. Receiving a good behavior letter serves as a motivator to both student and parents alike. It also indicates that you took the extra time to recognize that individual. One last idea for consideration would be using the *Teaching Personal and Social Responsibility Model* developed by Hellison (1978). The TPSR levels could be posted in the gymnasium. Students could self-assess to determine what level was indicative of their own behavior in class that day. The teacher might also choose to have students write out in their journals why they felt they were at a particular level. Students could set goals for themselves and determine some behaviors that they could employ to help them attain the desired level of personal and social responsibility that they wished to achieve. Students would be intrinsically rewarded as they met their goals. The model could additionally be employed to monitor whole-class behavior by the teacher and/or students.

In summary, many effective motivation techniques currently exist and are readily available for beginning physical education teachers. Take time prior to beginning the school year to devise a well-developed cadre of motivation techniques that can be used to establish a productive learning environment for the school year. Albert (1996) in her discussion about long-term encouragement strategies believes that fostering the three C's: (a) helping students feel *capable*, (b) helping students to *connect* with the teacher and fellow students, and (c) helping students *contribute* are essential keys to building student self-esteem.

Teachers can help students feel capable by: (a) making mistakes okay, (b) building confidence, (c) focusing on past success, (d) making learning tangible, and (e) recognizing achievement. Providing acceptance, attention, appreciation, affirmation, and affection are key elements to helping students connect. Finally, encouraging students' contribution to the class, school, and community; as well as inviting students to help other students are avenues worth pursuing in an effort to helping students to contribute. As you create and develop your motivational techniques repertoire, reflect on how the techniques might help students achieve the three C's.

Implementation

Once the classroom management plan is set and ready to go, the beginning teacher must determine how it will be implemented. Four questions should be considered as you begin to formulate the implementation of your classroom management plan. First, how will you *convey* the classroom management plan to your students? Second, what *problems or concerns* do you anticipate in establishing the management plan, and how do you plan to address them? Third, what will you do *initially* to enforce the management plan? And fourth, how well does your management plan reflect the *needs and characteristics* of your students and the school context?

In response to question one above, there are several means by which novice teachers can convey their management plan to students. A visual display or posting of physical education rules, protocols, consequences, and motivation techniques/incentives is perhaps the most-employed method of communication by experienced physical education teachers. Hand-in-hand with the visual presentation is the verbal description of the displayed information. As the teacher verbally communicates expectations, use of examples and non-examples can serve to clarify rules. Additionally it is important for teachers to provide checks of student understanding at various points throughout the communication of the classroom management plan. This could be accomplished by giving students a designated "behavioral scenario," while asking them to identify the misbehavior, as well as the resulting consequence. It would also be prudent to ask students *why* the behavior was inappropriate, and what *effect or impact* it might have on the learning environment. These types of discussions will help students understand why certain rules or protocols are put into effect. Students tend to be more compliant if the rationale provided for the rule makes sense to them. And, although it is advantageous for a beginning teacher to have the rules in place prior to the start of school, providing some student input is often beneficial and useful. A teacher might consider asking students if any additional rules are needed to provide for a good learning environment in which all students can learn. A little bit of student input can go along way in getting students to choose to behave in an appropriate manner. If they've been a part of creating the rules, they then become vested and, subsequently, are often less likely to violate the rules.

Alternatively, the classroom management plan might be conveyed by providing a written handout to students and parents. Often, physical educators provide students with a copy of the rules, protocols, expectations, and designated consequences. Students are then expected to take the handout home and discuss it with their parents/guardians. Generally, both student and parent/guardian are requested to "sign off," indicating the handout was read and understood by both parties. Consequently, students cannot use the excuse that they "didn't know" when a violation of rules or protocols occurs. Teachers can produce the signed form indicating the student (and parent) has a clear understanding of what is expected in the physical education classroom.

Finally, an important strategy to use in communicating a management plan is to actually *teach* the rules and protocols. Novice teachers tend to assume if they've posted a set of rules and procedures and they've talked about them, students automatically know how to respond accordingly. Providing activities that will assist the students in learning the rules and protocols is critical to achieving compliance. Practicing locker room procedures, entry into the gym, distribution and collection of equipment, and so forth, in concert with teacher expectations, will alleviate the need for continual reminders and subsequent delays in management later on.

In response to question two, a primary problem or concern of novice physical education teachers is that students will "test the boundaries." Students will want to know just how far they can go before misbehavior results in a consequence. They also want to know if the teacher is going to be consistent in application of the consequences. Hence, it is critical for beginning teachers to positively reinforce desired behaviors, while following through on a consistent basis with set consequences for inappropriate behaviors. Once students understand and know the limits, the testing of boundaries will likely diminish.

How to enforce the classroom management plan initially follows this same line of thought. "Don't smile until Christmas" is a statement often made to student teachers by university supervisors as interns prepare to embark on their student teaching experience. The same holds true for a beginning teacher. Be firm and fair consistently in the application of your classroom management plan. A teacher can always ease up later, if appropriate. However, if you try to be easy going in the beginning of your tenure as a physical education teacher, it will work against you. It's like trying to take candy away from toddlers—they're not going to give it up without a struggle or fight. Don't seek to be a friend to your students. They've already got plenty! Seek, rather, to be their teacher.

Finally, consider whether your recently established rules, protocols, expectations, and consequences are realistic. Can students be successful in following the management plan as designed, or are you being unrealistic? Are your expectations developmentally appropriate? Is the management plan aligned with the principles of demonstrating respect for self and others? Does the management plan assist in the development of student self-esteem? And, in sum, does your classroom management plan lead to a physical education classroom that is conducive to the learning of *all* students?

Chapter 3
Record Keeping

Several record-keeping techniques are available that beginning physical education teachers can use to track a variety of items: attendance, tardiness, dress, participation, discipline, assessment, in addition to other miscellaneous components. Designing a system that tracks this information in advance of the start of school will assist in the logistical nightmare that could occur due to large numbers of students that must be tracked by a single physical education teacher. Sometimes, as a physical educator, you teach every student within the school. The level at which you teach will dictate the type and amount of items that necessitate tracking. Documentation of these items will greatly enhance the amount of information the teacher can convey to administrators, students, and parents.

Routine Tracking Items

Attendance in physical education class is typically more important to track at middle and high school levels. Often, attendance is taken during every class period; and thus, an accurate documentation of student attendance is clearly important. It also assists the physical educator in being able to spot excessive absences. It may provide a red flag for the teacher in attempting to establish student attendance and its importance on a consistent basis. Since physical education is considered a "performance" subject, student attendance is a critical factor linked to the ability of students to perform successfully in class. In general, it is best to use a designated notation in the grade book to document students who are absent on a given day. I recommend the following symbol to document an absence:

I use a "back slash" to denote an absence because if a student comes in tardy, I can easily adjust my notation system to reflect the same as illustrated below:

The back slash with a perpendicular intersecting line serves as the tardy designation. Furthermore, one could denote whether the absence or tardy is considered excused (EX) or unexcused (UX).

The following abbreviations may also be helpful in formulating a grade book notation system:

E/X = Excused absence

U/X = Unexcused absence

ND = Not dressed

ND/NP = Not dressed; not participating

ID = Improper dress (some item of uniform is missing: shoes, shirt, shorts, socks, etc.)

NP/Ex = Not participating/excused

NP/Ux = Not participating/unexcused

M/Ex = Medical excuse

The notation system you employ must meet your unique needs. The samples provided are enough to get you thinking about what might work best in your particular context. Employing such a system will be beneficial in tracking several different measures on students in physical education. It will be important to provide a key to your notation system so that others are able to accurately identify all designated tracking measures at the beginning of the grade book. Typically, school grade books are turned in to the school at the end of the academic year. The school system keeps them for several years in case questions arise concerning student grades. Furthermore, many school systems have software programs in place to track many of these same features. Teachers may also use PDAs to accomplish record-keeping tasks as well. These provide an effective and efficient means of documentation, often reducing time spent in record keeping.

Behavior Management Tracking

In addition to some logistical and procedural tracking information, teachers may choose to track inappropriate behavior via the grade book as well. The notation "IB" can reflect inappropriate behavior. A numerical system to denote the level of inappropriateness could be used as well. For example, if a teacher needed to ask a student to be quiet while giving directions, it might be documented as follows on the specific date on which the behavior occurred: "IB/1." This reflects that inappropriate behavior occurred, and the student was issued a level one (least severe) consequence. Many physical educators are either choosing, or are requested by their school systems, to keep a discipline logbook documenting inappropriate behaviors that occur. The following components are typically tracked: (a)date, (b student, (c)behavioral incident, (d)immediate consequence issued, (e)student response, (f)follow-up action, and (g)future recommenda-tions. It is probably wise to section off the discipline logbook by classes. This is an excellent behavioral tool for any physical education teacher to employ. Often, without a comparable tool, it becomes difficult to recall specific behavioral incidents. This type of system allows for easy access to both documentation and review of behavioral incidents that have occurred within the physical education context.

Assessment Tracking

Finally, assessments provide key, critical components used in calculating or tracking student progress in physical education, and hence, must also be recorded within the physical educator's grade book. Teachers may wish to designate a specific area for formative assessments and another area for summative assessments. Moreover, it might serve well to group each type of assessment according to learning domain. This will provide easy access to interpreting a student's grade within designated learning domains. Finally, grade percentages used to calculate the final quarter or six-week grade should also be provided (if used), culminating in the final grade and grade percentage (or grade descriptor on the elementary level). Teachers may choose to use a computerized spreadsheet for this purpose. Formulas for deriving grades can be put in the spreadsheet, thus allowing for easy calcula-tion of grades. A beginning physical education teacher's grade book, if effectively organized, can serve the teacher well in tracking and document-ing the progress of even large numbers of students in an efficient and effective manner.

Figure 4 shows an example of a grade page using the notations described in this chapter.

Figure 4. Grade Book Example

Subject __Physical Education / 9TH GR.__

Period Beginning __1ST 9 Weeks__

Period Ending _____

MONTH		AUGUST												SEPT.												
DATE		16	17	18	19	20	23	24	25	26	27	30	31	1	2	3	6	7	8	9	10	13	14	15	16	17
NAMES		M	T	W	H	F	M	T	W	H	F	M	T	W	H	F	M	T	W	H	F	M	T	W	H	F
Adams, Jackie	1																									
Barry, Cheryl	2			IB/I				E/K					ND													
Casin, Kurt	3																									
Dorman, William	4																									
Edwards, Anne	5								E/K	E/K		NP/EX														
Fairview, Gracie	6																	ND								
Johnson, Beverly	7			ID										/												
Powers, John	8							IB/I																		
Smith, Katie	9										M/EX		IB/2		NP/MX											
Wilson, Mike	10							U/K																		
	11																									
	12																									
	13																									
	14																									
	15																									
	16																									
	17																									
	18																									
	19																									
	20																									
	21																									
	22																									
	23																									
	24																									
	25																									
	26																									
	27																									
	28																									
	29																									
	30																									
	31																									

Figure 4. (continued)

MARK DISTRIBUTION				DISTRIBUTION SEMESTER			

PE Journal (30)	Self-Assessment (15)	Teacher-Assessment (20)	Golf Score Card (15)	Golf Rules Test (30)	Speedball Rules Test (30)	Officiating/Speedball (5)	Off/Def Strategy (5)	GPAI – Golf (50)	GPAI – Speedball (50)	Golf Round (20)	Speedball Scoring (20)	Daily Average	Test	Period Average	#	1	2	AV	EX.	GR	Class Rank
21	12	20	10	27	26	4	3	40	48			17	15		1						
18	10	14	12	25	24	4	5	42	41			18	12		2						
30	15	15	11	21	23	3	3	38	42			15	10		3						
30	13	14	14	19	20	5	4	25	33			10	13		4						
27	11	19	15	30	28	5	4	44	41			11	12		5						
29	13	17	15	26	25	2	4	33	38			12	11		6						
15	12	17	8	24	27	3	5	27	30			13	10		7						
28	11	13	10	23	21	3	5	42	40			17	14		8						
30	15	20	12	17	20	4	3	39	43			19	10		9						
16	13	19	13	22	19	5	4	41	44			18	11		10						
29	14	19	13	25	24	5	5	44	45			18	12		11						
															12						
															13						
															14						
															15						
															16						
															17						
															18						
															19						
															20						
															21						
															22						
															23						
															24						
															25						
															26						
															27						
															28						
															29						
															30						
															31						

Category groupings: Affective (65) — Affective Total; Cognitive (85) — Cognitive Total; Psychomotor (140) — Psychomotor Total. GPAI – Speedball (50): Offense, Defense, Skills. Period Marks (1, 2, AV); Semester (EX., GR, Class Rank).

PART III - Go!

Once you've done all the necessary advance preparation prior to the start of the school year, it's time to set foot in your new school. Part III provides an orientation to the first few days of school for newly hired physical education teachers. It also discusses how to prepare the physical environment, as well as pertinent information on getting to know students, scheduling possibilities, and related supervision duties. Next, effective communication techniques relative to students, parents, and school personnel are presented, along with public relations and advocacy tips. Finally, teacher socialization factors are addressed.

Chapter 4
First Days of School

Getting Acquainted With Your School

The first days of school provide beginning physical educators with several opportunities. Generally speaking, most school systems require newly hired teachers to report to school in advance of returning faculty. Well-developed school systems provide a detailed and comprehensive orientation for new teachers, thus answering many questions and concerns that arise for new teachers. Similarly, many school systems also have what are known as "teacher work days" or "staff development days" scheduled prior to the arrival of students. These are typically designated for faculty preparation of classrooms, staff development, and instruction for the beginning of the new academic year.

Select school personnel. Getting introduced to office personnel and facilities staff is one of the first tasks at hand for beginning teachers. Office staff can be a valued and treasured asset within the school. They can respond to many common concerns of newly hired faculty members. If a teacher has a question, one of them most likely knows the answer or can refer the teacher to an individual that can appropriately address it. Furthermore, facilities staff has the potential to be key personnel to whom the physical educator can turn for advice on facilities and/or equipment. Since the physical education "classrooms" consist of both indoor and outdoor contexts, there are more opportunities for things to go wrong in terms of maintaining the physical environment. One of the best recommendations I can make to a beginning physical education teacher is to become well acquainted with the school facilities' staff (i.e., janitors, cooks, building maintenance personnel). Building a positive, working relationship with them will transcend many potential problems for years to come.

Likewise, office personnel are valuable and informative in assisting beginning teachers in tasks such as acquiring office supplies, learning how to use the copier (or procedures to request copies) and phone/intercom system, requesting needed supplies, as well as several other procedural routines. They will be able to address many beginning teachers' concerns as they work to become acclimated to the new job. Once again, these are key school personnel who assist in making a beginning teacher's transition easier and less stressful. The relationship established with school office personnel is a valuable one.

School policy handbook. One of the first items beginning teachers need to get in their hands is a school policy and procedures handbook. This will be the reference guide for all related policies and procedures set and established by the school system from teacher arrival and dismissal policies, teacher absence policies, emergency procedures (i.e., weather-related, fire), designated exit routes, student attendance policies, student dress code, general expectations of students, discipline code, to student injury procedures, and student medical information. Become familiar with it at once. As a professional, it is your responsibility to do so. Otherwise, the safety and well-being of your students may be at risk.

Medical concerns. As a physical education teacher, the potential for student injury is a legitimate cause for concern. Therefore, it is imperative to know specific emergency procedures that must be implemented in the event of an injury during physical education class. Documentation of an injury and details surrounding the circumstances leading up to an injury are crucial, no matter how minor the injury may appear. Most, if not all schools will have an "Injury Report Form" on file that the supervising teacher will need to complete. This should be done as soon as possible, while incident details are still fresh in mind. Similarly, schools designate set procedures for handling injuries resulting in bleeding. Specific protocol relative to this particular circumstance must be handled as prescribed by the school system. Failure to adhere to school policies and procedures with respect to injuries could result in potential negligence and/or liability lawsuits.

Physical educators, whether novice or experienced, must have access to student medical information as it relates to the physical education context. Allergies to grass, hay fever, bee stings; medical conditions such as asthma, diabetes, epilepsy; physical, developmental, or cognitive impairments; and medications relative to ADD or ADHD, among others can provide serious implications for those teaching physical education. Physical educators must be cognizant of each student diagnosed with a medical condition. Once informed, teachers are obligated to put into place appropriate procedures and strategies for how they will deal with specific types of medical emergencies relative to the medical conditions illustrated, in addition to others not previously addressed. These procedures may already be in existence at the school. If so, the beginning teacher must be ready to enact them at any time during instructional or supervisory roles. Discussing a plan of action with appropriate personnel (i.e., school nurse, special education teacher) will increase the likelihood of establishing proper procedures. Being prepared and proactive in advance will set the context for handling any medical situation that arises in an effective and appropriate manner.

School outlay. Finally, obtaining a school map outlining rooms, offices, and locations, along with designated exits will provide beginning teachers with a means of navigating the new territory. The complexity and diversity of the school outlay will be dependent upon many factors including size of the school, as well as its designation as either an elementary, middle, or high school building. Becoming familiar with the school outlay will reduce any initial anxiety in terms of where specific classrooms, offices, or any specialty areas such as the media center, gymnasium, lunchroom, and auditorium are located. In a short period of time, the new teacher will be able to maneuver the school as well as the veterans.

In conclusion, get to know as much as you can about the school, students, faculty, and staff with whom you'll be working. Refer to the Orientation Guide provided in Figure 5 (Bain & Wendt, 1983) for a comprehensive list of information and questions beginning teachers should seek responses to as they begin their new teaching assignments.

Figure 5. Orientation Guide to the New Teaching Experience*

I. General Information

A. Demographic Data

1. School system:
2. Complete school name:
3. Personnel director for school system:
4. If appropriate,
   dean of students:
   guidance counselor(s):
   department chairperson:
   athletic director:
   school nurse:
   head custodian:
5. Superintendent:
6. Principal:
7. Vice-assistant principal(s):
8. School board
   president: members:

Figure 5. (continued)

B. Teacher Requirement Data

1. Time teachers report to school?
2. Time teachers can leave school?
3. Are teachers required to sign in and out of school? Where?
4. Procedures teachers follow if sick or absent?
5. Will I be required to perform special duties such as hall, lunch, or bus duty?
6. What are the requirements for teachers relative to faculty mtgs., department mtgs., or extracurricular activities such as athletics, PTA, or open-house functions?

C. School Policy/Organization/Services Data

1. What is the general chain-of-command procedure to follow in discipline situations?
2. Are there special policies to follow for chronic absentees?
3. What are the procedures to report absentees in classes?
4. Are there special procedures to follow for tardy students?
5. Are hall passes or permission slips used? How?
6. Are homerooms scheduled in class? When?
7. What procedures are to be followed to arrange observations of other faculty in physical education and other classes?
8. Will I be allowed to use instructional resources, media equipment, and copier equipment and are there special procedures to follow for these?
9. What is the general socioeconomic background of the students?
10. What percentage of students are transported to school by bus?
11. Will I be given a student and faculty handbook and will there be a special orientation to the material within these handbooks? By whom?

D. Health/Safety/Accident Data

1. Is a school nurse on duty?

   Time: Days: Location:
2. What forms/procedures do I use if a student is injured in class?
3. Will I be instructed on plans for emergency evacuations?
   a. Fire drill procedure from gym/teaching station (procedure written up?).
   b. Disaster procedure from gym/teaching station (procedure written up?). (What are my specific responsibilities in the above situations?)
4. What types of daily/weekly excuses are accepted and how are they authorized?

Figure 5. (continued)

5. What procedures are normally followed when a student returns to class following an extended absence (injury or illness)?
6. Are there special resources for teachers to check out specific health/participation restrictions of students?
7. Are there parental permission slips sent home with students that state specific policy and safety rules to be acknowledged by both parents and the student for certain activities such as gymnastics, swimming, or track and field?
8. Ask yourself these questions:
   a. Did I check out all safety hazards in the teaching area to be used?
   b. Did I inform my class thoroughly of these hazards and related rules?
   c. Did I bring the attention of school authorities to possible hazards in my teaching area (in writing and retaining a copy)?

II. Physical Education Class Data

A. Policy/Procedures/Organization

1. Is there a departmental handbook for teachers to follow?
2. Is there a student policy/procedure sheet for students?
3. Is there a course of study (curricular guide/yearly curriculum schedule) available?
4. What type of attire are teachers required to wear during the teaching of classes?
5. What, if any, are the requirements for student dress in activity classes? Is this requirement used as part of their grade?
6. Pre-class phase/procedures.
   a. How are locks/lockers assigned?
   b. How are lost locks, equipment, and personal items handled?
   c. Are there special locker room procedures to follow? Supervision by whom?
   d. What is the roll call procedure used? Does it change with specific activities?
   e. Is there an opportunity for general pre-class activity before the instructional phase begins? Type of activity?
   f. Are classes started with the traditional exercise period? Or is there a special procedure for certain activities?
   g. Is a special check-out system procedure used to disperse equipment for both the teacher and student?
   h. What procedure do I follow to procure equipment for my units of instruction?
7. How are squads and/or teams designated? (Who makes up squads/teams?)
8. Will I teach as one member of a team-teaching approach? What activity? Duties?
9. What is the grading system used by the department? What are the areas of

Figure 5. (continued)

evaluated behaviors? Skills? Knowledge? Conduct? What is the weighting of these areas? How are grades reported to class? What code/symbol is used (P/F)? What options/limitations will I be given in grading my units of teaching? When are reporting periods? Are progress reports given out?

B. Staffing/Curriculum/Special Data

1. Will I be required to assist in extracurricular activities?

2. Will there be any inservice days for the department faculty? When? Where? What is the topic?

3. Are students with disabilities mainstreamed into all classes or just in a special activity or activities? (Find what limitations exist of those students mainstreamed into the class.)

4. Are special adapted (intact) classes scheduled separately for students with disabilities?

5. Will special education teachers assist in mainstreamed classes?

6. Are there any special handling procedures to use for students with disabilities?

7. What units of activity will I be exposed to during my experience and what units will I teach myself?

8. What type of daily lesson plan and unit plan formats am I expected to use? Are they to be examined? If so, when and to whom are they given?

9. Will I have available or be expected to use an instructional bulletin board?

10. Will I be expected or permitted to generate instructional study-guide handouts?

11. What professional education organizations does the school recommend I join when I begin to teach?

III. Athletic Responsibilities

A. Pre-season

1. Finalize my schedule and send a copy to all opponents. Obtain phone numbers, addresses, and schedules from all opponents. The state school directory will be of great help.

2. Run a strong conditioning program (under supervision if allowed).

3. Determine the first possible practice date and schedule gym time accordingly.

4. Organize a league or city-wide coaches meeting. Discuss rules, tournament policies and procedures, and selection of officials if this hasn't been set.

Figure 5. (continued)

B. In-season

1. Eligibility requirements. Is there a minimum GPA for participation as well as continual participation? School requirements? Interscholastic league requirements?

2. Does the school charge an athletic fee for participation on a team? What happens when a student is removed from the team?

3. Is the school going to provide practice suits or do the students provide their own?

4. Maintain a good working relationship with the athletic director and other coaches. Invite them to games.

5. Is there an attendance policy for practice and games?

6. Is a trainer available to be at practice and matches?

7. Can I have a team manager to assist with uniforms, prepare for home and away matches, etc.?

8. How is transportation arranged for away matches? What paperwork is needed and when is it to be filed? Do I have to serve as chauffeur? Who pays for a bus driver if one is used?

9. Will admission be charged for the home games? Does it go into a general fund? Who controls the use of the profits?

10. Who makes game-day preparations? Clocks, scoreboards, announcers, concession stands, ticket takers, officials, sweeping, and cleaning up after ward?

C. Off-season

1. How are equipment and uniforms ordered?

2. When is the budget submitted for the following year?

3. Set up an off-season training program and/or practice if allowed and feasible (gym space available).

4. Can I recruit within the school or in the district schools that promote into the school?

5. Begin securing next year's schedule and reserve gym time.

6. Is there a booster club that supports my group?

7. Can I raise funds for my team's use?

(Go back and answer ID and II as they relate to your coaching assignment.)

---

* Adapted from materials developed by Ronald Carlson, Indiana University.
Bain, L., & Wendt, J. (1983). *Transition to teaching: A guide for the beginning teacher* (pp. 5-8). Reston, VA: NASPE.

Getting the Physical Context Ready

Now that you've become familiarized with school personnel, policies and procedures, the physical outlay of the school, whom to see for what, you are ready to initiate preparation of the physical context. This may include a variety of aspects including, but not limited to, bulletin boards; gymnasium(s); office space; locker rooms and locker assignments; equipment room and equipment; outdoor facilities; placement and access to first-aid kits; as well as posting of class rules, protocols/daily routines, and consequences.

Bulletin boards. The use of bulletin boards provides a valuable mechanism by which teachers can convey varying types of information to students. In general, teachers of most subjects, including physical education, are designated bulletin board space on which they can communicate information to students. Bulletin board themes may vary from current topics in physical activity or sports, movement concepts and skill themes, fitness information, to ways to maintain or achieve a healthy, active lifestyle. The board may provide information about physical activity programs within the community (i.e., parks and recreation programs) that students learn about. Another option is to post the national standards in physical education, as well as the definition of a physically educated person. A teacher could then align curricular activities of the school physical education program with corresponding standards. This offers students a comprehensive and visual depiction of the physical education program.

Promotion of lifetime physical activity might serve as another potential theme. The possibilities are endless. One note of caution, it is recommended that bulletin boards be designed to convey physical education content to students, as opposed to statistics for the school volleyball team, etc. Typically, the athletic department can provide access to statistics in a designated location appropriate to the athletics' area.

Once you determine a theme, get to work on how best to convey and display the information. Good bulletin boards will meet the following criteria: They will (a) convey a colorful representation of the theme, (b) depict it in a creative manner, (c) capture the attention of students, (d) present pertinent information relative to the theme, and finally (e) communicate the information in a developmentally appropriate manner relative to age and grade levels of students. Finally, while the primary bulletin board audience is students, it will be visible to other faculty, administrators, and parents alike. Be sure it conveys the right message. It is your opportunity to advocate and inform others about physical education.

Gymnasium and indoor facilities. There may or not be a lot that the physical educator can to do to facilitate the preparation of the gymnasium itself for the arrival of students. Generally, floors will have been refinished or cleaned, dependent upon their composition. Beginning teachers should avail themselves of the opportunity to do a "once over" verifying that everything is in good working order. Physical educators may wish to check ceiling lights and get facilities staff to replace any bulbs that are burned out. Furthermore, checking to ensure bleachers and wall dividers are working appropriately is also recommended. In addition, basketball standards that raise and lower from ceilings should be tested to determine they are functional, showing no signs of technical difficulty. Rules, protocols/routines, and consequences, in addition to any specific safety issues, need to be posted and housed within gymnasium areas. This will provide students with a visual reminder of appropriate behavior and consequences that will occur for misbehavior.

With respect to specialty areas such as gymnastics, dance, or swimming facilities, generally a faculty member within the specialized area will be designated to monitor and maintain these particular types of physical education facilities within the department. Unless a beginning physical education teacher is an expert in one of these areas, he or she usually will not be required to perform this specific function. Finally, if a school has exercise or weight rooms, equipment within these designated physical education areas, in addition to the organizational set-up, must be checked as well for safety and any required maintenance.

Office. Office space availability will vary from school to school, but typically the physical educator's office space will be located close to the gymnasium and locker room areas. Moreover, several physical educators may occupy the same office space, based upon school design. Minimally, a desk, one or two chairs, and a file cabinet should be provided. If available, a bookcase and bulletin board would serve as further additions to complement a beginning teacher's immediate needs. Additionally, the beginning teacher will need various office supplies such as paper, scissors, scotch and masking tape, stapler, grade book, lesson plan book, paper clips, pens, pencils, sticky notes, and color markers. Many school systems provide these items on a routine basis. Find out in advance whether the school does so. If not, you'll need to get yourself started with some of the basics. If you need to purchase these items out of personal funds, save and document receipts for tax purposes. It is possible that you may acquire enough to qualify for a tax deduction for essential items not supplied by the school that you purchased specifically for professional use.

Nowadays, many physical education offices are equipped with at least one computer station. This can be a tremendous help, and there are numerous physical education software programs that can be incorporated as well. Ideally, at least one of the physical education offices will have direct access to a telephone. Due to the increased risk of physical injury, this becomes a critical item of necessity for the physical education context, particularly in the event of contacting emergency personnel should an injury occur. Finally, as you work to organize and arrange office space, you may wish complement it with some personal items (i.e., pictures, posters, calendar).

Locker room facility. The locker room facility is usually specific to middle and high school context. It should be cleaned and disinfected. Usually this task is delegated to facilities staff. Physical education teachers should ensure this has been accomplished. In addition, they may wish to prepare for student locker assignments. It might be beneficial to develop the master list of locks, with their respective lock numbers and combinations. It may be that this list already exists. If so, the teacher can put a lock on each locker to be used, noting the same. The master list should also have a column to designate the student assigned to the specific lock and locker. Additionally, it is a good idea to identify class period. Doing so will allow for an efficient tracking procedure should student locks become misplaced, or on the occasion of mistakenly putting someone else's lock on another student's locker. Finally, it is recommended that teachers post a separate set of locker room procedures in full view to provide a visual reminder of the same to students.

Equipment/equipment room. Readying the equipment room and physical education equipment for the start of the school year, as well as on a routine basis, is a key task delegated to physical educators. Organizing equipment according to use, amount, and easy access will provide physical educators with long-term benefits. If possible, all equipment should be stored off the floor on shelves, cabinets, cage box carts, etc. All equipment should be appropriately marked with either the school name or its initials and its designation as physical education equipment (i.e., YHS-PE). Physical education equipment needs to be checked in terms of both safety and usability. Are balls inflated to appropriate levels? Are nets in need of repair? Is hardware on equipment secure and in good condition? Any equipment that is found to be below standard should be replaced or repaired. Get rid of any equipment that is no longer safe for use. In addition, you may wish to check to see if an equipment inventory exists. If so, verify its accuracy. If one does not exist, initiate the process by developing an inventory list of your own. This will be of tremendous help in becoming familiar with amounts and types of equipment available for use, as well assisting in the determination of immediate and future equipment needs. Throughout the school year, maintain a list of existing needs, in addition to an equipment "wish list" that can be used in the development of a budget request for the following school year.

If the equipment room is located within the gymnasium, it provides a logical access point for a first-aid kit. Each physical education area should have a first-aid kit located for quick accessibility. In terms of outdoor facilities, if a storage area is adjacent to playing field space, this can serve as a potential location during outdoor physical activities. In the event that no storage areas are available for immediate access, it is recommended that a first-aid kit be transported with the teacher during physical education classes.

Outdoor facilities. Readying outdoor facilities for student use is one of the final preparation aspects to be addressed by physical educators. Again, facilities staff is often charged with maintenance of field areas. However, a key responsibility of physical education teachers is to ensure the safety of their students. Therefore, checking field areas for foreign objects (i.e., broken glass), obstructions, and uneven field surfaces, such as holes or divots that could possibly result in student injury is a necessity. Furthermore, outdoor facilities should be checked prior to the start of physical education classes on a daily basis as well. Finally, physical educators can use this time prior to the start of the school year to paint or chalk lines for specific outdoor physical activities (i.e., soccer, lacrosse, ultimate Frisbee) where feasible.

Getting to Know You

Upon arrival at a new school, it is important for the beginning teacher to become acquainted with his or her students, in addition to faculty, staff, and facilities. First impressions can directly impact the relationship that will be built between teacher and students. It will be particularly critical to get to know students, learn student names, and clearly convey classroom rules and teacher expectations in a short period of time. This will set the stage for a productive and quality teacher-student relationship.

First, organizing students in such a manner as to facilitate learning student names is tantamount for beginning physical education teachers, due to the large numbers of students that they will teach in a given year. Taking attendance can help in this process. Some physical education teachers choose to take attendance with students aligned alphabetically or numerically in a single line. Others prefer the use of squads instead. No matter what your preference, the key will be to determine an organizational format that works best for you. It will take time to learn student names; however, there are a few tricks of the trade that can expedite this process.

Teachers must make a concerted effort to learn student names. The sooner they are able to do so, the sooner they will gain control of their classes. Students tend to respond to teacher directives quickly if they are identified by name. And, once they realize the teacher knows their names on an individual basis, they typically choose to respond and behave in a more appropriate manner. Teachers can use name games to help them learn student names, particularly on the elementary level. These types of activities generally require students to call out their own name or that of another student when gaining or changing possession of a ball or some other object used in a low-organized game. Alternatively, teachers can conduct a variety of informal assessments on students. This is a great way to learn student names quickly. Another option available is requiring students to wear nametags initially, or enforcing the labeling of student names on physical education uniforms (if required). These actions will greatly assist in this challenging endeavor. You may also want to assign homework during one of the first few days of school, requiring students to write a letter to you. Ask students to share some information about them that will provide insight on their backgrounds and areas of interest. In addition, teachers could request information regarding likes and dislikes relative to physical education. Sometimes getting to know a little about your students on a personal level will assist you with developing a caring and quality relationship with your classes. A final suggestion to employ in learning student names is taking a minute or two either as students get organized for class to begin, or wait for dismissal. During this period of time, teachers can get to know something about a few of their students (including their names) through the initiation of informal conversation.

In addition to learning student names, it is important for teachers to begin to establish a good, working relationship with students. Team-building activities or challenges can serve as a terrific avenue to pursue in getting students to learn how to work with you and one another in a productive manner. Moreover, they can provide a foundation for establishing good social relationships among students if conducted effectively. Refer to Appendix B, Resources for Physical Educators, to acquire resources to implement team-building activities.

Teachers who become involved in school activities will reap the benefits at least threefold. Students enjoy seeing teachers at their various extracurricular activities. Teachers should attend a variety of school-related activities. Not all students are athletes. Those that aren't will appreciate your attendance at events in which they have an interest (i.e., chess club, drama, debate team). It lets them know that you share a genuine interest in them and what they do both inside and outside the classroom. It additionally offers you the opportunity to mention that you saw them at a designated event. This can help to develop a good relationship with your students. Participating in or attending many school activities/events provides teachers with the opportunity to explore student interests in the educational setting.

Teachers can also initiate some *icebreakers* at the start of the school year. The objective is to establish a comfortable, positive, safe, structured, and productive learning environment. Mr. Jon Evans, former student and current middle school physical education teacher finishing his second year of teaching, along with his mentor, Mr. Steve Marquis, were gracious enough to share their thoughts and ideas on how to set up a good working relationship between teacher and students, among other issues during a recent presentation at our student teaching luncheon. Let me share a few of their ideas here. One routine they establish in their class is to shake the hands of every student at the beginning of class. Initially, students are uncomfortable with this practice. But with time, they look forward it and begin to add their own unique type of handshakes. It lets students know they are important— each and every one of them. "People Search" is another activity that can easily be conducted at the beginning of a lesson. A handout is used in this activity; where students must identify a different person in the class to fit each description/question posed such as, "Find someone who has lived in another state or province. Which one?" or "Find someone who has won a contest. What kind of contest?" You are only limited by your own imagination in developing intriguing people search descriptions and questions. Be sure to provide one where you will be the only person to fit the description!

Sharing good news items or positive thoughts (i.e., Happy Birthday) are other available options that only take a few minutes at the start of a lesson. Another alternative is to conduct drawings or raffles from time to time for school supplies, library passes, dance tickets, athletic event tickets, etc. that are awarded to a lucky student. The goal is for the teacher to keep track of those who've won the drawing, and be sure that by the end of the year each student has been drawn as a "class winner."

Likewise, it is important for students to get to know you, as a teacher. Generally, it is beneficial for teachers to share a little about themselves in an effort to establish a productive relationship with their students. Keeping it simple will provide students with some basic information about you, without the need to get into too much detail about your life. Sharing information on your interests and hobbies provides an appropriate context in most cases.

More importantly, students will need to know your expectations. Teachers will want to establish and convey their expectations in a clear and concise manner from day one. This includes communicating rules, protocols or daily routines, consequences, and any additional expectations. To establish teacher expectations will sometimes necessitate practice of the same, particularly at the elementary school level. For example, it will be necessary to practice how students are to enter the gym, as well as where they are to go. Implementing start/stop signals, home base, distribution/collection of equipment are other examples that will often need to be taught as well as communicated. Once established and applied consistently, however, these routines and procedures will greatly diminish the amount of management time needed during a lesson. Additional information regarding the communication of rules and expectations can be found in Chapter 2, Developing a Classroom Management Plan.

Scheduling

The scheduling of physical education classes will typically occur prior to the arrival of new teacher hires. Hence, as a beginning teacher, you most likely will not have input into its design. Generally the principal, assistant principal, or an appointed committee of faculty and administrators will be responsible for schedule design. The number of times students are scheduled on a weekly basis for physical education and length of class period will vary greatly from school to school, as well as state-to-state. Often at the elementary level, physical educators teach approximately eight to ten classes a day; oftentimes, without any transition time from one class to the next. This can present a challenging experience for novice teachers with respect to organizational and equipment changes that may be required based on content covered. The number of times students have physical education on a weekly basis at the elementary school level will also vary, dependent on the individual school or school system.

Most middle and high school physical education classes will occur daily. However, there are exceptions to this rule. Several middle and high schools offer physical education/health as a single course; thus, students may rotate on a weekly or two to three-week period from health to physical education and vice versa. Other schools choose to conduct health and physical education classes on alternate days of the week throughout the length of the semester. This is often referred to as the A/B schedule. Operating under the A/B schedule, students would have physical education three days a week, and then rotate to two days of physical education the subsequent week.

Lastly, there are many schools that have transitioned to what is referred to as block scheduling (primarily middle and high schools). In general, a course that typically spans a full academic year is taught within a single semester. This is accomplished by teaching the course during a 90-minute block period. Block scheduling has both advantages and limitations with respect to physical education. On the plus side, it allows the opportunity for both fitness and skill development within the same physical education lesson without shortchanging either. On the down side, students only take physical education for one semester of the academic year; and therefore, it is anticipated that there may be a substantial decrease in the amount of physical activity during the semester in which physical education is not scheduled. Teachers who teach on the block schedule teach three class periods a day. In contrast, teachers on a traditional middle or high school schedule teach five class periods per day. Finally, teachers' schedules should provide for a minimum of one planning period per day. As the designation indicates, teachers use this period to prepare and plan for instruction.

As beginning teachers gain experience, they may wish to consider advocating for physical education to be taught to all students on a daily basis, if this is not currently the norm. The potential benefit to students is great. Conducting a quality physical education program at your school will provide the best opportunity to make a case in support of daily physical education. Collecting data that supports this position is equally important. In addition, an advocacy kit specifically designed for this purpose is available for teachers through NASPE.

Supervisory Responsibilities

Teachers often are delegated additional supervisory responsibilities above and beyond required teaching responsibilities. These may include, but are not limited to, locker room supervision, hall supervision, cafeteria or lunchroom supervision, and bus supervision to name a few. And, although most classroom teachers perform some type of assigned hall supervision as part of their responsibilities, physical education teachers are oftentimes delegated some share in the remaining responsibilities.

Locker room supervision is essential. Without it, there's a lawsuit waiting to happen. Leaving students unsupervised as they change clothes for physical activity can result in serious consequences as one can well imagine. Adult supervision must be provided. Schools that fail to do so are not acting in the best interests of their students in terms of providing a safe environment. If students dress for physical education classes (middle and high school levels) and your school does not currently employ such supervision, it is important for you, as the physical education teacher, to enlighten and educate your administration on the liability and negligence issues that this lack of supervision presents. Steps to remedy this supervision problem require immediate action on the part of all individuals concerned.

In addition to locker room supervision, cafeteria or lunchroom supervision and bus supervision are generally handled by physical education teachers. Policies and procedures (as well as resulting consequences) must be implemented and clearly conveyed to students in both contexts to ensure the safety and well being of students. This is particularly important with respect to bus supervision in terms of students boarding and exiting the buses. It will be necessary for beginning teachers to inquire as to their delegated supervisory duties, in addition to accessing designated school policies and procedures relative to each from school administration.

Finally, issues of safety and liability should be addressed by physical educators relative to both instructional and supervisory roles—on and off the field. Teachers should always be in the presence of, and directly supervising, the group or class. Students should never be left unattended for any reason. This pertains to coaching as well. The coach is ultimately responsible to ensure that all athletes have been picked up by parents or designated guardians prior to leaving the school building following a game or practice. Coaches should not only remain at school until athletes are picked up, but should directly supervise athletes until all have been accounted for. Schools must have back-up procedures to ensure there is always at least one or more teachers supervising at any given time, dependent upon number of students present, activity, student grade level, and risk of the activity. Teachers must also be aware of inherent risks and safety issues relative to physical activities. They must be able to properly instruct students in specific content to ensure for safe and appropriate performance. Equipment should be checked in advance for safety concerns and to ensure it is in working properly. General safety rules, as well as those specific to the activity must be addressed at the beginning and throughout every class as appropriate. It is also strongly recommended that a list of specific safety rules be posted in an area (i.e., gymnasium) that will serve as a continual, visual reminder to students. As a teacher, coach, or supervisor, it is important for you to know your students well. Be cognizant of the extent of their capabilities and gear instruction and supervision accordingly. Students must always know that you are in direct control (Siedentop & Tannehill, 2000).

Chapter 5
Keeping the Lines Open- Effective Communication

Keeping the lines of communication open, in tandem with effective communication are two essential skills a physical education teacher must possess. Teachers communicate on a variety of levels. Primary communication occurs with students. However, teachers also communicate with parents, school personnel, and the public in general via public relations and advocacy efforts. Communicating inside and outside of the classroom in an effective manner can be key to developing a successful physical education program.

Students

Physical educators communicate with students for a variety of purposes. They communicate with students to: (a) provide instruction, (b) offer feedback, (c) give reinforcement and encouragement, (d) manage student behavior, (e) question for understanding, and (f) challenge, to name a few. And, since most beginning physical education teachers spent a great deal of time and effort on each of the above types of teacher communication during their respective teacher education programs, I will refer to forms of communication not often experienced previously by new teachers prior to the start of their first teaching position.

As a beginning physical education teacher, it will be important to convey the physical education curriculum students will be exposed to over the course of the academic year, as well as how it relates to subsequent years in their school system (elementary, middle, and high school). Students should be informed about types of physical activities they will be pursuing, as well as why. Additionally, it is essential for teachers to communicate how these specific activities will lead to achieving stated student-learning outcomes. Doing so provides students with a more holistic perspective of the school physical education program. Teachers can subsequently relate resulting benefits to be gained by participating in the same.

Likewise, teachers must communicate student progress and performance toward achieving targeted learning outcomes. This can be accomplished in a variety of ways via formative and summative assessments. Formative assessments are particularly valuable to students as they seek to improve performance, knowledge, and behaviors. In this respect, they receive communication on their progress throughout a unit of instruction, rather than at its culmination. Typically, middle and high schools issue student progress reports that provide students (and parents) with input regarding progress during the first half of a grading or marking period. This provides an opportunity for students to continue to improve over the second half of the designated reporting period. Teachers are able to inform students of where they stand and what they need to do to maintain or improve their performance and grade prior to the end of the marking period. In general, progress reports are sent home either with students or through the mail. Parents are requested to sign the progress report, indicating they have reviewed it, and subsequently return it to the school.

Report cards, commonly issued at six- or nine-week intervals, communicate information regarding how well students performed for a specified marking period. As stated previously, elementary school reports cards generally use a descriptor (outstanding, good, satisfactory, or needs improvement), while letter grades are standard at middle and high school levels.

Beginning teachers may also choose to communicate student progress through use of formal or informal written notes. Many teachers use this as a positive reinforcement for appropriate behavior during class. Or, if a student is working particularly hard over the course of a period of instruction, the physical education teacher may choose to recognize this type of effort as well. Most students enjoy receiving these types of notes that recognize efforts put forth during physical education class. Oftentimes, teachers will use certificates, or a form letter that allows them to write in the particular behavior or performance to be recognized. It is a good idea for teachers to use discretion in the number of good news notes they choose to send to students, so that their effect doesn't become minimized. In fact, teachers can track students that have received such recognition in an effort to attempt to send one to every student at some point during the academic year.

With the latest release of information on childhood obesity as communicated by the Centers for Disease Control and the U.S. Surgeon General, it becomes particularly critical for physical education teachers to provide maximum physical activity during instruction. Moreover, it is known that students need to participate in additional physical activity outside the context of physical education in order to achieve a sufficient level of physical activity. It is the teacher's duty and responsibility to communicate and expose students to programs available, in terms of extracurricular school physical activities (i.e., intramurals, athletics), as well as community programs (i.e., parks and recreation, afterschool programs). While athletic programs provide opportunities for students who are physically adept in specific sports, community programs are geared toward individuals who would like to learn more about a sport or physical activity without the need to be accomplished prior to entering the program and thus, are designed for the general population. Communicating and exposing students to these opportunities aligns perfectly with NASPE Content Standard 3, "exhibits a physically active lifestyle" (National Association for Sport and Physical Education [NASPE], 1995).

While most communications discussed up to this point consisted of written or verbal communication, nonverbal communication with students can convey very powerful messages as well. A nod, or thumbs up can communicate a positive message, just as well as a teacher's verbal positive reinforcement to a particular student. Teacher disapproval can also be noted in a similar way (i.e., giving the "eye"). Both forms of nonverbal communication can be effective. The key to appropriate use of nonverbal communication for beginning teachers is to make sure it is consistent with what the teacher communicated to students either verbally or in written format. Incongruent messages will more than likely cause confusion in students' interpretation of the teacher communication.

While all the communication thus far has been described in terms of teacher communication, it is crucial that teacher and students can also effectively communicate and interact with one another. Asking questions to check for student understanding will provide beginning teachers with a fairly good indicator as to whether the message has been clearly communicated to students. Teacher observation of student response to a teacher communication (i.e., directions for a specific learning task) will also provide a clear picture as to whether students received the message as the teacher intended. Additionally, asking for student input where appropriate can be a tremendous asset in developing a rapport with your physical education classes. This is a powerful vehicle for developing a positive and productive learning environment if handled in an appropriate manner. The more students are able to provide input, the more they become "vested" in the program and class.

Teachers should design their programs to provide this type of communication and opportunity to occur. Relationship building with students is clearly a critical key to establishing good rapport.

Communication can be crucial when dealing with a confrontational situation. Beginning teachers must learn how to communicate effectively on these occasions, particularly student-teacher confrontations. Albert (1996)

Table 9. Guidelines for Confrontation*

Guideline 1: Focus on the behavior, not the student

- *Describe the behavior, don't evaluate it.* Provide an objective, rather than subjective, description of what happened.
- *Deal with the moment.* Only consider what is happening at the moment. Don't bring past events into the situation.
- *Be firm and friendly.* Be firm about the misbehavior, but friendly toward the student (still show genuine concern).

Guideline 2: Take charge of negative emotions

- *Control negative emotions.* Avoid allowing students to get the best of you.
- *Release negative emotions.* Vent in an appropriate location (perhaps with a trusted colleague) after the event is over.

Guideline 3: Avoid escalating the situation

- Avoid doing or saying things that will make the situation worse (i.e., raising voice, degrading, physical force, preaching, backing student into corner).

Guideline 4: Discuss misbehavior later

- Designate a later time (when both teacher and student have cooled off) to discuss misbehavior.

Guideline 5: Allow students to save face

- If students are not allowed to save face, teachers risk provoking a new confrontation.

* Adapted from Chapter 8 of the *Cooperative Discipline Teacher's Handbook* by Linda Alberts © 1996. American Guidance Service, Inc., 4201 Woodland Road, Circle Pines, Minnesota 55014-1796. Adapted and reproduced with permission of publisher. All rights reserved. www.agnet.com.

provides five guidelines for teachers' use in de-escalating confrontations with students. These provide beginning teachers with a general format and guide to follow when this type of problem presents arises. Refer to Table 9, Guidelines for Confrontation (Albert, 1996), for a detailed description.

Lastly, teacher communication with students should be fair and consistent, both in terms of instructional and managerial aspects. These will provide a basis for students to respond to teacher communications clearly and appropriately. Sending inconsistent or mixed messages will only lead to problems on the ability of students to understand and respond accordingly.

Parents

Many teacher communications with parents consist of those previously or simultaneously communicated to students. Teachers should communicate the physical education curriculum and its goals to parents. They should also convey intended student learning outcomes. Similar to students, parents are then informed of what the school physical education program is attempting to accomplish with respect to their children. In addition, parents are informed of student progress in physical education toward stated learning outcomes through student progress reports and report cards.

Along these same lines, it is appropriate for teachers to communicate their classroom management plan to parents as well, so parents are informed of teacher expectations, behavior guidelines, and consequences. While both curriculum and management components may be addressed to parents through written communication, oftentimes there is an opportunity to communicate the same verbally during school open houses typically conducted within the first week or two of the start of the school year. Being able to address the parents as a group on these items, along with a written handout/letter provides an extra opportunity to interact with parents in the school context.

Beginning teachers may also want to solicit help from parents in conducting parts of their physical education program. I remember one experienced physical educator that recruited "motor moms and dads" to work with his elementary school physical education program on Fridays. He would use the "assistants" in a variety of ways (i.e., fitness testing, field days, various motor assessments). And, although this type of recruitment is generally conducted at the elementary level, there may be occasions when physical educators at middle and high school levels can take advantage of some type of parent expertise in physical activity or related areas. Furthermore, providing an open invitation to parents to drop in during your physical education classes can assist in strengthening the teacher-parent relationship as well.

Most importantly, beginning teachers need to take the initiative to keep parents informed in terms curriculum, student progress/grades, behavior management, and so forth. One wise Disney Teacher of the Year, Ron Clark, emphasized the importance of having the first contact with a student's parents/guardians be a positive one. Parents and guardians will be more receptive to future teacher communications if the first contact is positive. Moreover, maintaining an open-door policy with parents/guardians to learn about the importance of physical education and what their children need to do to stay physically active is critical. Providing parents with avenues to pursue with their children to lead healthy, active lifestyles will be appreciated as well. In many instances, these become win-win situations. Both students and parents gain more in terms of increased amounts of physical activity within their normal routine, in addition to providing for more family time. Parents can be the best advocates for your physical education program if you take the time to communicate effectively.

The parent-teacher conference is one area of communication that does not get developed until one assumes a teaching position. Generally, schools conduct parent-teacher conferences immediately following the first grading period of the academic year. It is best for beginning teachers to be well prepared for these conferences. This can be greatly facilitated if teachers have a variety of assessment measures previously conducted on their students, as well as weightings for various components calculated into the grade. In addition, some parents may be interested in their child's behavior and/or attitude during physical education class. Maintaining a log of discipline incidents will assist in verifying student behavior for this very purpose. Parent-teacher conferences also provide opportunities for teachers to question parents with respect to how their children learn best, or for ideas in terms of how to motivate their children or achieve behavior compliance during physical education classes. Physical educators should strongly encourage students to have parents attend parent-teacher conferences. Doing so will provide another opportunity to illustrate what a quality physical education program is all about, and what the physical education teacher is doing to help children become physically educated.

Finally, keep the lines of communication with parents open. If you are experiencing problems with a particular student, it is important to communicate this to the parents or guardians as soon as possible so that the problem may be appropriately addressed before it gets out of hand. Seek solutions to the problems that are being experienced. Often, parents can provide insight into what will and will not work with their children. Try to conduct a few "good news" phone calls, in addition to the "bad news" ones—particularly for those students who are typically challenging. Although it is seldom done, it can do much to reinforce the parent as well as the student. "Successful first-year teachers say parental involvement in education—at home and in the classroom—is vital to effective learning and discipline" (DePaul, 2000, p.12).

School Personnel

As the new "rookies" on the block, beginning teachers will have many occasions to seek advice and interact with faculty, staff, and administrators. Included within this diverse group are principal and assistants, fellow teachers, teacher aids, department chairs/supervisors, secretaries, facilities staff, cafeteria workers, and bus drivers. Take the opportunity to get to know everyone who works at your school, and allow them to get to know you. Establishing sound working relationships will certainly be worth the beginning teachers' while.

However, there is one note of caution to beginning teachers along these lines—the faculty/staff lounge. While this may appear to be the best place to get to know your fellow colleagues, you may wish to limit the amount of time spent there. Some teachers can be very negative about specific students, and this is often conveyed to others within the confines of the faculty lounge. Beginning teachers should be wary of formulating biases or prejudices on students based on conversation that originates in the faculty lounge. It is in the best interest of beginning teachers to give all students equal opportunity to succeed in their classes. Beginning teachers should not infer that because one teacher has problems with a particular student, they will encounter these same problems. Students are individuals and as such, they respond differently to different types of teachers. Oftentimes, students that typically cause behavioral and academic problems in subject areas of a more cognitive nature will excel in courses of physical performance (psychomotor domain emphasis), such as physical education. Don't make judgments based on another individual's evaluative comments. Give students the opportunity to be judged solely on their performance, knowledge, and behaviors exhibited in your physical education class.

In conclusion, beginning physical education teachers would be wise to follow the golden rule—"Do unto others, as you would have them do unto you." What better guide than this is available for both novice and veteran teachers?

Public Relations and Advocacy

It is important for beginning teachers to use public relations techniques to improve the visibility of their school physical education programs whenever possible. Parents, community, government officials, and so forth need to be informed about the importance of physical education in the schools, as well as how physical education programs are addressing such needs. Establishing such a support base for your physical education program will be of great benefit in maintaining and improving the program that currently exists.

This can be achieved in numerous ways; however, I will restrict comments to two potential avenues. The first strategy that can be used in promoting physical education via public relations is the establishment of a monthly physical education newsletter. Create a catchy title for it. Include highlights from specific physical activities (along with some photographs) that students have been working on at various grade levels. Include student comments that address positive outcomes achieved through these same physical activities. Introduce the public to the national K-12 standards in physical education. Illustrate how physical education standards have been addressed in the past month. Include a monthly calendar of daily physical activities that students and their families can do together. Perhaps promote some type of competition regarding the same. Share NASPE's definition of a physically educated person. Provide information tidbits relative to aspects of fitness and wellness, as well as lifetime physical activities. Provide current information from Centers for Disease Control and the Surgeon General, while making the connection to how it relates to your school physical education program. Put in requests for used sports equipment that families and businesses may be willing to part with for the benefit of supporting your program. Involve local sporting goods businesses in this endeavor as well. Here again, teachers are only limited by their imaginations relative to potential topics and benefits that will result from such a publication.

A spin-off of the newsletter strategy is the development of a web page for your physical education program. Monthly newsletters could also be posted and archived on this web site. Curriculum and program goals can be listed, along with the alignment to state and national standards. Creating quick links for easy access to issues on related topics in physical education, wellness, fitness, nutrition, exercise, and comparable sites provide a fast track to informing the public. You may decide to get assistance from students in creating and maintaining the website. Or, let a particular grade level develop a web page that could be highlighted on the physical education home page. These are just a few ideas that can get you thinking about the possibilities that exist in such a project. The potential is overwhelming.

A second avenue to pursue in the quest to inform the public about your physical education program is to have an open house specific to physical education. This should be a hands-on session for the public. Your students could take them through the paces. Expose the public to a variety of physical activities that are components in your physical education program. Demonstrate appropriate warm-up activities and exercises. Illustrate through hands-on experience what the "new physical education" is all about. Demonstrate the potential of a program that does not just "roll out the ball." Communicate the importance of daily physical activity in everyone's lives. Invite local TV stations and newspapers to participate. This will extend exposure above and beyond the limits of the open house. Lastly, the NASPE Advocacy Kit provides a wide array of additional recommendations physical educators can implement in support of their physical education programs. Be proactive with your physical education program. Don't take a back seat and risk losing what you have. Work on building a program that is better than ever.

Chapter 6
Socialization Factors

Beginning physical education teachers, in addition to their counterparts in other disciplines, are often challenged by the socialization process that occurs during their first teaching position in a school system. This process, or lack thereof, may be one of several factors leading to the vast numbers of beginning teachers choosing to leave the field of education after less than five years. It is difficult for beginning teachers to understand the complexities of school culture and subsequent socialization factors impacting them until they actually begin their first teaching position.

School Culture and Context

One of the first things beginning teachers should attempt to understand is the organizational structure of the school. The school is comprised of several subsystems including school administration, support staff, teachers, and student support services. Refer to Figure 6, School Organizational Structure, for a visual representation. These subsystems interact with activities that occur as a result of such subsystems including administering, teaching, maintaining, learning, creating, and socializing.

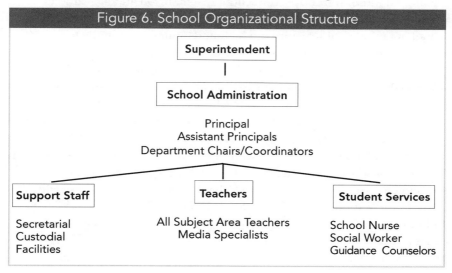

Figure 6. School Organizational Structure

Within schools there can be several layers of administration. The principal is considered to be the chief executive officer. Assistant principals serve in various capacities as designated and directed by the principal. Support staff and student services personnel report to the principal or designated assistant. And, in general, there is a department chairperson or a specific subject area coordinator that teachers report to, dependent upon subject area and school designation as elementary, middle, or high school. Media specialists are usually included in the teacher category as well. Support staff includes personnel responsible for secretarial, custodial, and facilities services. In contrast, student-support services include individuals whose primary roles are to meet the varied needs of students, above and beyond traditional teacher roles. This organizational element is comprised of, but not limited to, the following individuals: school nurses, social workers, and guidance counselors. Regardless of the school level at which you are employed as a beginning teacher, it is critical for you to see the relationship among these various elements of the school organization, as well as their roles and designated activities in relationship to your own.

If you are teaching at an elementary school, your first direct chain of command is more than likely the principal or assistant principal. At the middle school level, there may be a coordinator who serves as your first contact person in the chain of command. And, the department chairperson is generally the teachers' first contact person in the organizational hierarchy at the high school level. It is important to work within the chain of command established within your respective school system. If you are unclear as to whom this individual is, seek clarification as soon as possible. Usually the school organizational structure can be found outlined within the teacher/school handbook, with a clearly delineated chain of command. Determining roles and responsibilities designated by your teaching contract, and how they relate to the rest of the school will assist in defining who you are and where you fit in the complex scheme of your school organizational structure.

A school's organizational structure will usually dictate amount and type of power and/or authority granted to any particular position, in addition to its networks of affiliation. "Power involves control over others and is reflected by control of access to valued resources and dispersal of rewards and punishment. Authority refers to power that is accepted by others as legitimate" (Bain & Wendt, 1983, p. 27). School administrators have positional authority and power that is considered legitimate. Beginning teachers must carefully examine how school administrators operate within their roles. How do they make their decisions? Is faculty input welcomed or limited in scope?

By what method is it best communicated? What other factors impact types of decisions made? And, most importantly, how will decisions impact what you do in the role of teacher? A beginning teacher will spend the first year of teaching acquiring a good sense of the school organizational structure and the resulting socialization process that occurs.

Establishing a Support System

Some teacher education programs currently initiate a year-long internship experience, where interns spend one full day a week at an assigned internship site during the semester prior to student teaching. Such programs allow preservice teachers opportunities to investigate and explore school culture prior to assuming the intense demands that student teaching incurs. Thus, when teacher candidates do begin the student teaching experience, they've already been at least partially indoctrinated into the school sociocultural system, hence easing transition to student teaching. And, while this process is not available for beginning teachers, the majority of school systems have come to recognize the importance of providing a mentor for the beginning teacher, generally throughout the first three years of teaching. Ideally, the mentor will teach the same subject area in the same school as the beginning teacher. Mentor teachers are typically experienced teachers who can serve as resources, guides, and facilitators for beginning teachers. Their role is not evaluative in nature, but rather to assist beginning teachers as they learn how to be effective and successful during the induction phase of teaching. It will be critical for you to establish a good, working relationship with your mentor.

Sometimes, particularly at the elementary school level, a beginning physical education teacher may be assigned a mentor from another subject area. And, while this mentor can be a great support in terms of school policies and procedures, it might be wise to request (or negotiate) a second mentor from a nearby school who is a physical educator. Physical education teacher mentors are attuned to the specific context in which the subject matter is taught. Students do not sit in desks, but are generally moving throughout various phases of a given lesson. Organizational, managerial, behavioral, and instructional aspects that need improvement will be more evident to physical education teachers as opposed to classroom teachers. Finally, content knowledge and pedagogical knowledge as it relates to the psychomotor domain and developmental level of students is critical. Those not trained in physical education will not necessarily be able to discern what is developmentally appropriate in terms of both content and progression. So, if you find yourself in such a situation, work with school administration to arrive at a compromise that will afford you the best opportunity for success and support.

The mentor will work with you in a coaching-type role. He or she will assist you in gaining a better understanding of your school context, students, other faculty, administration, and related personnel. If you are in proximity to your mentor within the structural setting of the school, he or she becomes your immediate contact person for questions, concerns, and problems that may arise. Remember, the mentor's job is to assist and support the beginning teacher during the initial indoctrination into the school system. Use your mentor well. If you have questions regarding school policies and procedures, or need to know who to seek for answers to questions, the mentor becomes a good place to start.

The mentor is more than just a question-and-answer person. He or she will also help you determine areas of teaching in which you excel, and those needing further development. Often, mentors will assist in the development of an "action plan" or "professional development plan" to address specific aspects of your teaching effectiveness. In addition, mentors can serve as role models for beginning teachers. For example, mentors can model select teaching skills or strategies to be practiced and further developed by beginning teachers. Mentors can also assist in various aspects of planning and instruction, while serving as a sounding board for beginning teachers as they search to find strategies, approaches, and techniques that are effective and fit their personal style in the teaching world. Mentors can help beginning teachers establish a record-keeping system, as well as guide in the establishment of a grading and assessment system. Moreover, mentors may spend a great deal of time with beginning teachers initially as they fine-tune and implement the classroom management plan.

The mentor is a beginning teacher's primary base of support. Establishing a good relationship with this individual can be crucial in determining the level of success you will experience as a beginning teacher. Learn as much as possible from your mentor, as well as other colleagues and school personnel.

Likewise, you will wish to solicit other colleagues to become part of your support system. If there are other physical education teachers at your school, you will usually be drawn to them, since you will work more closely with them on a day-to-day basis and you share the same context and subject area. Some of your counterparts will provide a terrific support system, while others may not. Seek to develop strong relationships with physical educators that hold a similar teaching philosophy comparable to your own. Seek out those who are true physical education professionals. Look for physical educators who are up-to-date in terms of content, curriculum, and standards, as well as developmentally appropriate practices. Physical educators who attend workshops and conventions on a regular basis are generally current in terms of the profession. Look for faculty who are motivated and demonstrate enthusiasm in their teaching—those always seeking ways to do things better. Search for colleagues reflective about their teaching, and search out those who are genuinely concerned about students and their learning.

While it is important to foster relationships with physical educators who are committed professionals, also seek to establish relationships with faculty outside your subject area. Look for similar qualities to those mentioned above. This will assist you in gaining a better perspective of other subject content areas. Likewise, colleagues will acquire a more comprehensive understanding about physical education and its role in the school as well. Moreover, this may lead to opportunities to work with individuals on interdisciplinary content development.

In contrast, work diligently not to be adversely influenced by others, particularly physical educators who may pressure you to conform to their teaching practices, which may mean no teaching whatsoever, but rather "rolling out the ball" (ROB). This practice backs novice teachers into difficult situations. First, beginning teachers demonstrate a need to be liked by their colleagues. Second, they need to be able to work with them. Third, some of these faculty have probably been using the ROB technique for years and have little, if any, desire to change. After all, if you teach appropriately and effectively, they begin to look slack. This can cause numerous problems. Beginning teachers need to hold firm in their efforts to provide students with the best physical education experience available. As a physical education teaching professional, it is your responsibility to help students develop adequate and ideally competent physical skills, knowledge, and beliefs/ attitudes, in order to increase the likelihood that they will choose to stay (or become) physically active throughout their lifetimes.

Choosing to be different from the rest (those who use the ROB technique) will not be easy. It will take courage and perseverance on your part as a beginning teacher. You may decide to demonstrate that what you do in terms of teaching is of benefit to your students. You may even be able to convince a few colleagues that what you're doing makes sense. Some experienced physical education faculty may be interested in your results; however, usually beginning teachers will find that many of the experienced teachers have already made their choices, and generally they are not willing to attempt alternative approaches. In fact, in many school systems, physical education teachers are held more accountable for their coaching than teaching. Sometimes, as long as they are winning, they're not held accountable for their teaching at all. It's a sad, but true, statement, and does not speak well to those physical education professionals who do their job in an appropriate manner.

You can begin implementing change, if necessary, one step at a time. Do not attempt to turn the department or program upside down. Instead, proceed wisely and carefully. Back up what you know to be true with evidence. Start by implementing one or two instructional units as you perceive they should be conducted. However, do this with students that are new this year to the school system. In other words, if you teach at the middle school level (grades 6-8), begin this change with sixth graders—they know no different, since they are just beginning the middle school experience. It is a lot easier to initiate change in this manner. That is not to say you should not try to initiate change with grades seven and eight. However, your approach should be much slower in progression and transition. Initially, you may need to negotiate your way with students who have been previously exposed to another system. Be patient and proceed slowly. Then, let the fruits of your efforts speak for themselves.

Your students will also have a great deal of impact on you in the school socialization process (Schempp & Graber, 1992) as might be expected. If students have experienced the ROB technique, understand that it may take a substantial amount of time before they decide to accept the beginning teacher's physical education agenda. Some students will more than likely resist, at least initially. After all, it's been fairly easy for them thus far. As long as they dressed out and didn't cause any problems, they received an easy "A" in physical education. Believe it or not though, there are a lot of students who would prefer to do something other than play basketball day in and day out. These students would welcome the opportunity to participate in a variety of physical activities. In summary, any initiation of change will take time and patience for students to respond appropriately. So, be diligent and steer your curriculum on the right course.

There are a variety of other issues often faced by beginning physical education teachers. They include (a) reality shock, (b) isolation, (c) marginalization, (d) workload and role conflict, and subsequently (e) de-professionalism (Mohr & Townsend, 2001). In brief, reality shock occurs when a beginning teacher's first position is quite different in context than that which was experienced during student teaching. Many times physical education teachers (comparable to band, art, music) find themselves isolated both graphically in terms of location within the school, and also with respect to opportunities to interact with other faculty. Marginalization refers to stereotypical perceptions frequently associated with physical education and its teachers. Physical education is often viewed as a *marginal* subject or less important than others, such as math, science, or reading. Other subject area teachers' and sometimes school administrators' comments and actions reflect this marginalization. For example, physical education teachers are frequently the last to be notified that their teaching space (gym) will be used for an assembly. And sadly, some teachers believe the only reason for including physical education in the curriculum is so that other subject area teachers can get a planning period.

Role conflict and workload are also typically problematic for beginning teachers. Ideally, beginning teachers should not assume any type of extracurricular responsibility. They really need to spend their time in planning and preparation, particularly during their first years in teaching. However, contrary to that statement, many beginning physical education teachers would not have been hired for teaching positions had they not agreed to coach at least one to two (sometimes three) sports during their first year of teaching. Finally, de-professionalism refers to succumbing to status quo—reverting to the path of least resistance, which generally means choosing to give into pressures faced, and perpetuating the chronic problem of rolling out the ball.

Some PETE programs provide induction support services at the college/ university to recent graduates of their programs. This may be set up formally (seminars, workshops) or informally (individual faculty, contacts). Alternatively, listservs, message boards, distribution lists, and other means of technological communication allow for contact and support without the need to travel.

It is crucial for beginning teachers to position themselves for success. Build a good network of support. Interact with professionals who are passionate and dedicated to teaching. Continue to grow professionally (refer to Chapter 7, Professional Development). Choose to provide students the best possible physical education program within your resources. Physically educate your students to the best of your ability.

Community

Beginning physical education teachers must not only be socialized into the school, they must also be socialized within the community as well. If beginning teachers are not members of the community in which they teach, they need to make a concerted effort to get to know the community on a fairly in-depth level. What types of businesses/commerce are present within the community? What is the community's socioeconomic status? Is the community diverse? Is it urban, suburban, or rural? How involved is the community currently within the school system? Are there opportunities that could serve as potential resources with respect to the physical education curriculum? Hopefully, your mentor will have answers to many of the above questions. Perhaps you investigated the school system in advance of interviewing for the position and were able to get an adequate grasp of the community. If not, search out individuals who can help to get you started. Then, begin establishing relationships within the community at large. The potential benefits will definitely be worth the effort.

PART IV - STAYIN' ALIVE: SURVIVAL AND DEVELOPMENT

Now that you've been introduced to aspects necessary to establish an effective classroom, as well as interaction and socialization factors, it time to reveal other opportunities and considerations that await you as you embark on your first teaching position. Part IV begins by discussing professional development opportunities. Suggestions are then offered on how to maintain balance in juggling personal and professional roles as a beginning teacher. Various topics such as team teaching and the health education classroom, along with suggested possibilities for future projects are highlighted as well. Finally, insights and concluding remarks are offered.

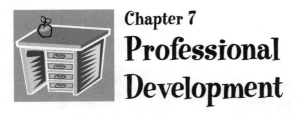

Chapter 7
Professional Development

Professional Organizations

One of the best ways for a beginning physical educator to "stay alive" is to become a member of one or more professional organizations directly linked to the licensure area. The professional organization most clearly linked with physical education is the American Alliance for Health, Physical Education, Recreation and Dance (AAHPERD) in association with the National Association for Sport and Physical Education (NASPE). Acquiring membership in AAHPERD, along with association in NASPE, is your lifeline to the profession with outstanding benefits. First, membership entitles you to select one of four practitioner and research-oriented journals: *JOPERD – The Journal of Physical Education, Recreation, and Dance, Journal of Health Education, Research Quarterly for Exercise and Sport,* or *Strategies.* You will also receive AAHPERD's newsletter, *Update* six times a year. Workshops and conferences for practitioners (teachers in the field) are offered regionally and nationally. Recently, AAHPERD implemented a new service for members entitled, "Pipeline" that provides opportunities to bring workshops to local school systems. Furthermore, AAHPERD also represents the best interests of the profession from local levels through national levels, as an advocate for quality daily physical education. Through its recent lobbying efforts, NASPE/AAHPERD was able to see through funding and passage of the Physical Education for Progress (PEP) Bill, sponsored by Senator Ted Stevens of Alaska. The PEP Bill authorizes $400 million dollars over a five-year period for grants to local education agencies in efforts to provide for quality physical education programs. Joining AAHPERD/NASPE keeps you current in physical education research, standards, and practices. It informs you of appropriate practices and related physical education publications. It is an excellent resource as you begin your career as a physical education teacher. Refer to the membership form at the back of this text if you are not a current member.

In tandem with AAHPERD, it is recommended that you join your state and district AHPERD organizations. This provides a closer-to-home connection. Typically, state and district AHPERD organizations publish a journal or newsletter at regular intervals throughout the year. In addition, they annually host a state/district convention. AAHPERD conventions at state, district, and national levels are some of the best you can attend as a professional. They provide numerous presentations and workshops for K-12 practitioners, in addition to marvelous networking opportunities with other physical education professionals like you. You can also interact with a host of exhibitors (i.e., physical education equipment vendors, Jump Rope for Heart representatives, book publishers, innovative software merchandise vendors). All of these provide exceptional avenues to continue professional growth and development throughout your teaching career.

Continuing Your Education

Although most beginning teachers recently completed their undergraduate degree, at some point in time, returning to the university to obtain a degree at the master's level makes a great deal of sense. There are several avenues that can be used to accomplish this task. An individual can choose to pursue work on a master's degree full-time. Typically, under these circumstances, one is unable to teach, or chooses to substitute on a part-time basis, while working on the graduate degree full-time. Alternatively, physical educators will choose to continue their full-time teaching positions in the K-12 schools, while pursuing the advanced degree on a part-time basis. This is feasible at many institutions, particularly in teacher education. One barrier to initiating the graduate degree is coaching. Often, practice and game schedules offer no consistency over the course of a given semester; and consequently, can make it quite challenging for a teacher/coach to successfully complete the advanced degree.

However, if the opportunity is available and feasible, it is recommended that teachers, upon completion of the induction phase of teaching, work toward a graduate degree usually in the area in which the professional is currently teaching (i.e., MAEd in Physical Education Pedagogy). Continuing formal education in the licensure area will provide for an intensive and in-depth coverage of content, theory, research, along with its related implications for instructional practice (i.e., action research). It will expose teachers to the latest and current trends and research in numerous content areas including: instructional approaches/models, curriculum, planning and instruction, class management, effective teaching, and assessment aspects. For teachers whose nearest college or university is too far away to travel to, several online programs offer an alternative path. Often universities organize online degree programs that distance students can complete concurrently with onsite students. And, although some online programs exist without any face-to-face coursework, other universities complement the distance-learning component with several weeks on-site during summer sessions to incorporate a component of the traditional form of coursework and interaction among university professors and fellow graduate students. Therefore, travel distance no longer limits an individual's ability to pursue and obtain an advanced degree in a designated area of preference.

Opportunities also exist to pursue and achieve certification as a "master teacher." The National Board of Professional Teaching Standards (NBPTS) now offers this avenue of achieving national recognition in the physical education teaching profession. In order to be eligible to apply for national board certification, teachers must have a minimum of three years successful teaching experience. Teachers choosing to pursue national board certification are put through a rigorous application process that is quite complex and requires several months to complete. Included are designated portfolio entries as related to the NBPTS standards, in addition to a series of assessments candidates must complete at designated testing centers. Each component is weighted, and cumulative totals of both portfolio entries and assessments are calculated to determine whether the national board teacher candidate has achieved national recognition status. This certification process provides an unbelievably intensive, reflective, professional growth experience for teachers pursuing this exceptional opportunity.

Lastly, for those with summers available for professional development purposes, Human Kinetics offers American Master Teacher Program (AMTP) workshops for teachers who wish to continue professional development in physical education. The AMTP was developed by George Graham in an effort to provide additional opportunities for physical educators to hone teaching skills and to encourage developmentally appropriate practices in physical education. These workshops are conducted for several days and include both theory and practice (hands-on) components, ultimately leading to a certification test offered the last day of the workshop. Again, this recognition provides current physical education teachers with another avenue for professional growth and development.

Professional Development Goals and Action Plan

All teachers, whether novice or experienced, should set professional development goals or outcomes, along with a strategic action plan to assist in attaining targeted outcomes on a yearly basis. Goals and outcomes should be set at the beginning of the academic year. This may be a formalized process in the school system. If not, it is something that should be done for continued professional growth and development over time.

Development plan to improve teaching. One goal beginning teachers may wish to target initially pertains to specific aspects of teaching effectiveness. Consider what teaching strengths you possess as you begin your first official teaching position in the schools. Next, evaluate and reflect on teaching aspects/skills that necessitate further development. Develop a list and prioritize specific areas you'd like to improve, refine, and further develop. It may be that as a beginning physical educator, you are concerned with how your lesson time is spent relative to instruction, activity, and management. If so, this would be an appropriate aspect of teaching on which to focus. Subsequently, set a targeted outcome that is both measurable and observable for one or more of these three lesson components. For example, "I will provide at least 65% to 75% activity time, while reducing management time to no more than 8% in any given physical education lesson taught."

You may choose to use Randall's (1992) Systematic Observation of Time Management Instrument to document progress on your selected teaching focus. This instrument allows teachers to track activity, instructional, and management time in a relatively easy format. Next, develop a list of strategies, approaches, and techniques to assist in reducing management time while increasing activity time within the lesson. Also determine how you will track progress on the selected teaching skill. Will you ask a colleague to complete the systematic observation instrument during some of your lessons? Or, will you videotape lessons and conduct the analysis on your own? Perhaps you will do a combination of the two. Regardless, it is suggested that you continue to focus on a single teaching skill until it is consistently within range of your targeted outcome, rather than attempting to focus on the improvement of several teaching skills simultaneously. In general, you will discover that focusing on a single teaching skill will subsequently demonstrate improvement in other aspects of your teaching as well (Senne, 1997). Refer to Figure 7, Development Plan to Improve Teaching Effectiveness, for a copy of the designated action plan.

Systematic observation for effective teaching. Systematic observation instruments provide an exceptional means to investigate, track, or document teaching effectiveness, with minimal training needed. There are a variety of types and formats available for use. They range from very simple, focusing on a single aspect of teaching, to very complex instruments that depict and document a wide range of teaching and/or student behaviors all in a single instrument. In addition, systematic observation instruments are

Figure 7. Development Plan to Improve Teaching Effectiveness

Development Plan

1. Select one specific **teaching behavior** from the list provided below (or another of your own choosing) that you wish to further develop over the course of the academic year. Circle or highlight the teaching behavior you have selected, or propose your own.

- Time Management Observation Instrument (TMOI)
- Planned Activity Check for Evaluating Lesson Effectiveness (Time on Task)
- Behavior Management Observation Instrument (BMOI)
- Maximum Practice Opportunities
- Student Task Success Rate (STSR)
- Positive Reinforcement Observation Instrument (PROI)
- QMTPS
- ALT-PE
- Other: _____

2. Write a **teaching outcome** for your selected teaching skill focus. The teaching outcome must be both *measurable and observable*. This outcome indicates how well you want to be able to perform the selected teaching skill. Once this goal has been attained (consecutively over the course of *several observations*), select a new teaching skill and write another development plan (number each development plan sequentially).

Teaching Outcome:

3. Develop a list of **several strategies, resources, and/or techniques** to be used to assist you in reaching your targeted teaching goal or outcome:

   a.

   b.

   c.

   d.

4. What specific **types of evidence** will you provide to **document** your progress in achieving your goal? What other types of evidence might you be able to provide for support in documenting improvement on your selected teaching focus?

designed to track not only teacher behaviors, but student behaviors (or student responses to teacher behaviors) as well. Many systematic observation instruments track specific measures using duration, frequency counts, or through some type of coding system, in addition to a variety of qualitative features.

Teachers can use systematic observation instruments in several ways. First, they can use the instruments as originally designed. Teachers can also modify existing instruments to provide additional or more in-depth information on respective teaching behaviors. Furthermore, teachers can create or develop systematic observation instruments that are tailor-made to their own specific preferences. Refer to the Appendix A, Selected Systematic Observation Instruments, for a variety of systematic observation instruments from which to choose.

Select teaching behaviors were found to have a more direct impact on student learning (academic achievement) than others (Walberg, 1986). Walberg found the following teaching behaviors to have a strong impact on student learning: classroom atmosphere morale, use of positive reinforcement, higher-order questioning, use of advance organizers, engaged academic learning time, cues and feedback, and cooperative learning activities. Once beginning teachers have fine-tuned organizational and managerial skills, teachers may wish to consider focusing on specific teaching behaviors that are noted to have a more direct impact on student learning. In sum, all teachers should use both formal and informal measures to track and document their teaching effectiveness on a regular basis as they attempt to continue to grow in the area of teacher effectiveness.

Teaching Portfolio

Teaching portfolios are currently used in a variety of ways, serving numerous purposes in the field of education. Most teacher education programs require teacher candidates to develop and construct teaching portfolios as one of the culminating projects in the degree program. In addition, many states are implementing some version of the teaching portfolio as a performance-based means of determining continuing teacher licensure. Of what benefit is it to you as a beginning teacher to develop and maintain a teaching portfolio?

It can be a tool that enables you to make sense out of a myriad of experiences. It also can bring into focus a clear picture of yourself as a growing, changing professional. Equally as significant, it can be a convincing, effective vehicle for you to demonstrate to others in a meaningful way the skills and knowledge you have gained in something as complex as teaching (Campbell, Cignetti, Melenyzer, Nettles, & Wyman, 1997, p. 3).

Teaching portfolios can be organized in multiple ways. Some teachers choose to use Interstate New Teacher Assessment Support Consortium (INTASC) standards as the framework for development and organization of their portfolios. INTASC standards are beginning teacher standards that serve as the measure by which programs and states determine teachers' competencies relative to each standard and its respective outcomes. For each standard, teachers provide evidence to document or demonstrate their competence with respect to the related standard and its outcomes. Thus, the portfolio sections would be organized based on the INTASC standards. Refer to Table 10 for a brief description of INTASC standards.

Table 10. INTASC Standards

Standard 1 – Content Pedagogy
The teacher understands the central concepts, tools of inquiry, and structures of the discipline he or she teaches and can create learning experiences that make these aspects of subject matter meaningful for students.

Standard 2 – Student Development
The teacher understands how children learn and develop, and can provide learning opportunities that support a child's intellectual, social, and personal development.

Standard 3 – Diverse Learners
The teacher understands how students differ in their approaches to learning and creates instructional opportunities that are adapted to diverse learners.

Standard 4 – Multiple Instructional Strategies
The teacher understands and uses a variety of instructional strategies to encourage student development of critical thinking, problem-solving, and performance skills.

Standard 5 – Motivation and Management
The teacher uses an understanding of individual and group motivation and behavior to create a learning environment that encourages positive social interaction, active engagement in learning, and self-motivation.

Table 10. (continued)

Standard 6 – Communication and Technology
The teacher uses knowledge of effective verbal, nonverbal, and media communication techniques to foster active inquiry, collaboration, and support interaction in the classroom.

Standard 7 – Planning
The teacher plans instruction based upon knowledge of subject matter, students, the community, and curriculum goals.

Standard 8 – Assessment
The teacher understands and uses formal and informal assessment strategies to evaluate and ensure the continuous intellectual, social, and physical development of the learner.

Standard 9 – Reflective Practice: Professional Growth
The teacher is a reflective practitioner who continually evaluates the effects of his or her choices and actions on others (students, parents, and other professionals in the learning community) and who actively seeks out opportunities to grow professionally.

Standard 10 – School and Community Involvement
The teacher fosters relationships with school colleagues, parents, and agencies in the larger community to support students' learning and well-being.

Another way to organize the teaching portfolio is to use the following section components and contents (Senne & Rikard, 2002), some of which are based on the former North Carolina Performance-Based Product for continuing teacher licensure. These sections address INTASC standards; however, multiple standards are addressed within a single section focused on a specific aspect of teaching. The first section, "Getting to Know Me," serves as an introduction to the portfolio. Within this section, teachers include a short autobiography, resume, and teaching philosophy. Section two, "Instructional Practices," focuses on INTASC Standards 1, 2, 4, 6, 7, and 8. This component is comprised of an instructional unit plan and subsequent lesson plans, a videotape of a lesson conducted during the instructional unit, and an analysis of the videotaped teaching episode. In addition, the teacher provides at least one form of student assessment in each of the three learning domains (psychomotor, cognitive, and affective) and includes samples of student assessment data. An analysis of student assessment data would also be included. Furthermore, this section would contain a directed reflection focusing on various aspects of instruction relative to the unit of instruction. Section three, "Classroom Climate," primarily focuses on establishment of a productive learning environment, relative to INTASC Standard 5. The teacher's classroom management plan (rules, daily protocols, consequences, intervention strategies, preventive behavior management, and motivation techniques), in addition to a discipline log or individual student case study relative to classroom behavior would be appropriate contents for this portfolio section, followed once again by a directed reflection. Section four, "Reflective Practice/Professional Growth," focuses specifically on INTASC Standard 9. Within this section teachers might include a copy of their "Development Plan to Improve Teaching," along with completed systematic observation instruments documenting progress and improvement on selected teaching behaviors/skills. Teachers might also choose to include documentation relative to attendance at workshops or conferences to complement the teaching behavior focus. Of course, a reflection specific to professional growth would be appropriate as well. Teachers may choose to include additional portfolio sections. Additional sections might include: diversity in the classroom, technology, coaching, photo album, collaboration with community, professional development, and parental involvement.

One of the most salient benefits of developing a teaching portfolio is the continual focus on self-evaluation and reflection (Senne & Rikard, 2002). Experiencing the process of developing a teaching portfolio can facilitate tremendous growth. Reflecting deeply about one's teaching practice leads to growth and subsequently, more effective teaching. Portfolio development is extremely time intensive and requires good time management skills, particularly if the portfolio is a required component of the induction process. Furthermore, developing a teaching portfolio during induction years will likewise prepare teachers for the challenging experience of attempting National Board Certification in physical education.

Conferences and Workshops

Conferences and workshops provide welcome opportunities for professional development. Workshops and conferences are often conducted by the state department of public instruction for teachers and target numerous aspects of the teaching/learning process and curriculum and instruction components. Locally, county or school district systems provide inservice workshops to address teachers' specific needs (both in content areas and in education in general), or to introduce teachers to new, innovative approaches in the field of education. And, as stated previously, workshops and conferences are also conducted specific to the discipline of physical education. These include annual AAHPERD conventions conducted at state, district, and national levels.

It is important for beginning teachers to avail themselves of workshop or conference opportunities. These avenues keep teachers current in the field, while providing additional training and development with respect to new and innovative educational initiatives and programs. Moreover, they allow for the forging of new professional and collaborative relationships with colleagues on several levels. Lastly, these opportunities get teachers "fired up" and motivated to continue to grow and develop in their teaching abilities, which ultimately benefits the student learner. Beginning teachers should seek funding to support continuing education endeavors, workshops, and professional conferences through the local school system. Oftentimes, money is budgeted for these types of professional development opportunities.

Professional Listservs

While workshops and conferences provide teachers with a forum to discuss and share educational initiatives, listservs offer this same opportunity via Internet-based discussion groups of teachers with common interests. This forum is accessible any time of the day, provided a teacher has access to the Internet. There are numerous listservs to which teachers can subscribe to share insights, problems, and innovations to the challenges teaching presents. One of the most visible listservs for K-12 physical education practitioners is the NASPE-L listserv. For information on how to subscribe to NASPE-L, go to the following website: http://listserv.vt.edu/cgi-binwa.cgi?SUBED1=naspe-l&A=1. Likewise, The Physical Education Forum (http://www.pelinks4u.org/discus/) is a message/bulletin board developed to stimulate interaction on topics of interest among professionals in physical education, health, sports, and fitness. Listservs and bulletin boards provide a tremendous opportunity to discuss and share concerns, as well as innovative solutions to challenges encountered by physical education teachers. They widen the network of opportunity by allowing interaction among professional colleagues in physical education across the nation at virtually any time of the day. Furthermore, they assist in keeping teachers up-to-date on the "pulse" of issues and challenges facing physical educators in the classrooms today, in addition to providing a forum to generate solutions to these same issues and challenges. Lastly, they can serve as a support mechanism, which is so critical particularly to novice teachers.

A few pointers are in order for maintaining membership in various listservs without going crazy. First, it is recommended that beginning teachers begin with one listserv initially. Although most listservs have transitioned to a digest format, teachers can still become overwhelmed by the amount of e-mail that can be generated by a single listserv. Subscribing to a single listserv initially will keep things manageable for the beginning physical education teacher. To subscribe, you e-mail the specific address listed for this purpose and follow the procedures outlined to subscribe. Generally, you will receive an e-mail stating your interest in joining the listserv to which you must confirm your intent within a 48-hour period. Upon doing so, the listserv will provide a document that outlines and describes procedures for posting, replying, subscribing, and unsubscribing, along with general etiquette for maintaining membership on the listserv. It is a good idea to print and save a copy of this document for future reference. Maintaining a file with such information will provide you with easy access in terms of the how to's of that particular listserv. Once you've read daily postings, either delete them or create a personal folder in which to file those you wish to have direct access to. Additionally, if you will be on vacation or not have access to the Internet for an extended period of time, it is recommended that you unsubscribe until your return. This will help you to avoid becoming inundated with accumulating e-mail postings from the listserv so that your e-mail account does not get out of hand and become unmanageable.

In summary, numerous professional development and growth opportunities exist for beginning teachers including: professional organizations, formal education options, conferences, workshops, and listservs. Self-development in the area of professional growth can also be fostered through a focus on improvement in selected teaching skills and portfolio development. Critical, in-depth reflection upon one's teaching is the crucial mechanism consistent across all professional development opportunities for beginning physical education teachers. Professional growth cannot occur without it.

Chapter 8
Maintaining Balance

Teaching/Coaching Conflict

In general, beginning teachers have their hands full just in terms of tackling their respective teaching responsibilities. However, most beginning physical education teachers also take on the additional role of coaching, as a counterpart to their teaching positions. This delegation of additional coaching responsibilities for physical educators is the norm, rather than the exception to the rule. And, beginning physical education teachers will usually choose to accept additional coaching responsibilities to ensure securing a position in their licensure area.

Coaching, in addition to maintaining a full-time teaching position is an enormous task, even for the most experienced physical educator. As such, it becomes extremely challenging for the beginning teacher. As a beginning physical education teacher, you will be spending a large component of time planning for instruction. This is a very painstaking experience, particularly during the initial year of teaching. Numerous factors impact instructional planning: class size, content, developmental level, skill level, available equipment, maturity level, social interaction level, and so forth in determining and planning what's most appropriate for the first year of classes. In addition, as a coach you will then need to plan for practices and game play relative to your designated coaching assignment. And, although you may have had prior experience in that same sport, appropriate planning for practices will also consume a good chunk of time.

So, how does a beginning teacher maintain balance in this dual role? First, remember what you're getting paid to do. You are first and foremost getting paid to teach. Whether the school system keeps you accountable for student learning or not should not matter. It is up to you as a physical education professional to keep yourself and your students accountable for student learning. Use the planning period for what it's designed. Prepare your lessons. Planning ahead will be of tremendous help. Instructional planning, as stated previously will account for the majority of work you will need to dedicate your time to as a beginning teacher. It will be of utmost importance to carefully plan your use of time. Becoming a good time manager in this dual role is critical. The beginning teacher must separate out these two roles from one another. Moreover, it is imperative to separate out the responsibilities of each role (teaching and coaching), to ensure you do not plan coaching practices during your daily planning period or during instructional time. The coaching duties and planning for the same will need to occur outside the regular school day.

As stated previously, the dual role is quite challenging, even for experienced teachers. If feasible, assume an assistant coaching position. It will provide the opportunity to be delegated less responsibility, while still learning coaching essentials under the direction of a head coach. Furthermore, agree to coach no more than a single sport during the induction years of teaching (years one through three) if at all feasible. Once you've gained some experience, you will be better prepared to assume a second coaching role, should you so desire.

Teaching/Personal Life Conflict

As a beginning teacher, you may also feel overwhelmed in terms of balancing out the teaching role with your personal life. Both deserve quality time. However, it can become quite a juggling act. Whenever possible, try to not bring home "school work" that needs to be completed during the evening. Some teachers do this by not leaving school at the end of the day until things are all set and in place for the next day's lessons. Consequently, when teachers go home, they can take time for themselves, family, or significant others. The principle "do school work at school" will assist beginning teachers in achieving some sense of balance in the midst of a juggling act. All of us need personal and/or family time, apart from our jobs. The goal is to keep both aspects separate from one another and attain quality time in both the job and personal aspects of your life. It requires beginning teachers to wear two different hats. The work hat comes off at the end of the day when one leaves school and the personal hat takes its place.

Beginning teachers may find themselves overwhelmed to the point that they can't see how to fit in any personal time. If you get to this point, it is necessary to carefully re-evaluate priorities and expectations. Your mentor might be able to assist you in achieving a better perspective relative to the personal and professional life. Beginning teachers, like experienced teachers, must achieve a sense of balance in juggling the professional role with the personal role. Failure to maintain balance will likely result in detrimental impacts on both roles. Watch for "red flags" or warning signs to appear. For example, bringing work home to do night after night with little or no time for family, friends, or yourself would be a good indicator that things are beginning to get out of balance. If there is no time for you to do as you wish, frustration will build. This frustration may also carry over into the workplace; and consequently impact your work as well. This makes for an undesirable situation that must be dealt with. It will necessitate that you re-evaluate, reflect, and modify your current patterns accordingly. Perhaps you will still need to spend some time on school work at home. If so, compromise and work only one to two nights a week, delegating the remaining nights for personal time doing whatever you find relaxing and worthwhile.

Common Sense Stuff

Finally, in order to achieve balance in life, focus on keeping yourself in the best physical and mental condition possible. Start with preventive measures that can be applied in order to stay in good shape physically and mentally—sound mind, sound body. The goal is to be able to function at your ultimate capacity. This will enhance both personal and professional aspects of your life. Begin by getting a sufficient amount of sleep and rest during the work week. Seven to eight hours of sleep per night on a regular basis is a primary key to success on the health and wellness front.

Nutritional aspects can also play a major role in maintaining your health. Include each of the food groups (breads, fruits, vegetables, dairy, protein, fat) in your daily eating regime. Avoid fast foods and quick fixes whenever possible. Planning out meals in advance will reduce the need for fast food trips. Bring healthy snacks (fruits, peanuts) to work to munch on between meals. Reduce the amount of carbonated and caffeine-type beverages. Drink plenty of water and take a daily multivitamin.

Most importantly, designate a time each day for exercise and physical activity. This is truly one of the best things that you can do for yourself. It will increase your energy level, make you feel good, and reduce stress, not to mention all the additional derived health benefits. This needs to be a priority in your daily regimen. As a physical educator, it is very important to model (or practice) what you preach. Others, including your students, will notice the rewarding results.

Finally, when you are feeling overwhelmed, prioritize. Attack items requiring immediate attention first. Break big projects down into smaller, doable parts. Consider developing a timeline with respect to determining which parts must be completed by a designated date in order for the entire project to be completed in a timely manner. Maintain a to-do list with deadlines to assist in staying organized, and use a daily planner to closely monitor activities and tasks that need to be done that day. Review tomorrow's schedule the night before to verify that all things are in order for the start of the next day. In sum, create and maintain a good organizational plan and manage your time well.

All of the above topics are what I refer to as *common sense* things. And, although they may seem basic in nature, adhering to the principles illustrated will do a great deal to help you become the most successful physical education teacher that you can be. You will not be the only benefactor of maintaining a healthy and active lifestyle.

Chapter 9
Possibilities

This chapter will briefly introduce beginning teachers to several topics relative to teaching physical education within K-12 school systems. Among topics to be considered are team teaching, cultivating connections and collaboration with the community, the health classroom, enhancing physical education equipment, school wellness programs, intramurals, and advocacy for physical education. While several topics may go above and beyond the scope of general responsibilities of beginning physical education teachers, it is important to consider these as potential possibilities for future endeavors.

Team Teaching

Often, team teaching is conducive to the physical education setting, particularly when there is more than one physical education class scheduled in the same facility (i.e., gymnasium) during the same class period. There are several advantages to team teaching. First, teachers are not competing with one another in terms of being able to verbally deliver their instruction. Second, students' attention is not drawn to what the other physical education class is doing. Third, there will most likely be better use of space and equipment by combining classes. Fourth, while one teacher is directing a component of the lesson, the other has the flexibility to move around the classes, providing both feedback and behavior management when needed. Fifth, students often enjoy the opportunity to have more than one teacher for instruction.

Despite numerous benefits of team teaching, some disadvantages exist and should be considered prior to choosing to team teach. Probably the most challenging aspect of team teaching is planning for instruction. In team teaching, teachers must coordinate lesson objectives and activities with one another. This often takes a longer period of time than would be necessary for a teacher to plan an individual lesson. Teachers must also be in alignment philosophically with one another in terms of unit objectives and learning activities, as well as assessment issues. Both will have to agree to the same content on each of these instructional aspects. Furthermore, teachers will need to be able to communicate and interact effectively with one another for this instructional approach to be successful. Beginning physical education teachers will have to weigh benefits against the limitations prior to initiating a team-taught unit of instruction. Above all, the needs of student learners must be kept as the number one priority in rendering this decision.

Cultivating Connections and Collaboration with the Community

Beginning teachers may also want to begin to discover potential sources within the community whereby collaboration could occur between the school physical education program and various community resources at large. A physical education teacher may wish to initiate an instructional unit that can't feasibly be taught within the school's facilities. The physical education teacher could seek out potential community resources or businesses that may be able to provide appropriate facilities. For example, it may be possible to conduct a unit in bowling at the local bowling alley. Perhaps some instruction from an amateur or professional bowler could be an additional highlight to the unit of instruction. Likewise, many cities and towns have indoor inline skating rinks. It might be possible to work in collaboration with the rink owner/manager and arrange for use of the facility, along with rental skates, and possibly some instruction as well. These types of initiatives in physical education provide students with an opportunity to experience some choices in physical activity that they may not otherwise be able to access at school. Moreover, these types of physical activities provide avenues for lifetime physical activity, and introduce students to uncovering resources within the community to facilitate this goal.

The Health Education Classroom

Teaching licensure (physical education, health education, or combined health and physical education) will directly impact the comfort level beginning teachers will possess in teaching health education content. If beginning teachers have little or no preparation in health education, but are expected to teach the content regardless, it may be in their best interest to take courses to acquire add-on licensure in health education. No matter what your particular situation is relative to teaching health education in addition to physical education, you must acquire necessary content knowledge and pedagogy to be effective in delivering the content. Seeking resources in health education might be a good place to start. If your colleagues currently teach health education, perhaps one of them could mentor you. Joining a professional health education association, such as the American Association for Health Education (AAHE), an AAHPERD association, would also be constructive. The *Journal of Health Education* is an available journal choice as a member of AAHPERD. Beginning teachers could choose association membership in both NASPE and AAHE. Attending conferences and workshops in health education can serve as another avenue to pursue in developing your knowledge. Additionally, there are many Internet resources available on health education lesson plans. Refer to Table 11, Health Education Lesson Plans, Links, and Resources, for a list of the same. Be sure when using Internet resources to verify that the information you have is accurate. The bottom line in terms of teaching health education is to gain skills and competencies necessary to provide students with the most accurate and effective teaching.

Table 11. Health Education Lesson Plans, Links, and Resources

- http://www.pecentral.org/lessonideas/health/healthlp.asp
- http://education.indiana.edu/cas/ttforum/lesson.html#health
- http://www.askeric.org/cgi-bin/lessons.cgi/Health
- http://www.healthteacher.com/
- http://www.pbs.org/teachersource/health.htm
- http://www.teachers.net/cgi-bin/lessons/sort.cgi?searchterm=Health
- http://www.edhelper.com/cat55.htm
- http://www.teach-nology.com/teachers/lesson_plans/health

Enhancing Your PE Equipment

There are several ways to enhance your physical education equipment supply. First, and most importantly, take good care of what you've got. Try to budget replacements for current equipment over several years, so that some is replaced annually. That way, not all soccer balls, for example, will need to be replaced at the same time. In addition, store equipment properly to improve its longevity. Taking proper care of equipment will assist in getting as much as you can out of your equipment budget. You or your department should submit a budget request for physical education equipment on an annual basis. Taking inventory at the end or beginning of the school year will assist in determining the most pressing needs. Typically, a rationale needs to be included with budget requests, in addition to approximate costs for each type of equipment requested. It is very important to use the entire dollar allotment for physical education equipment each and every year. If not, you will most likely be allocated a smaller budget in subsequent years.

Physical education equipment can also be acquired in alternative ways. Physical education teachers might send a letter home with students asking for used athletic equipment that's lying around or collecting dust on the shelves or in the storage shed. Teachers will be amazed at the amount of equipment they can acquire by employing this simple technique. Or, beginning teachers might create a "Physical Education Equipment Wish List." Elementary physical educators can make use of a variety of generic household products such as clothespins, plastic jugs, and so on. One elementary school physical educator I know collects stuffed animals from his students. He uses these when introducing catching as a skill theme. Stuffed animals are motivating to catch, and they don't hurt when you catch them! There may be some parents at home with craft skills that might be willing to make yarn balls. Here again, teachers are only limited by their imaginations. Furthermore, teachers can seek resources from businesses within the community. Local carpet stores are great places from which to acquire carpet squares to use in elementary physical education classes. Local sporting goods stores may be willing to provide used equipment (i.e., golf clubs) as well. And, the local Parent Teacher Association (PTA) may be willing to donate a portion of money raised to contribute toward funding new physical education equipment. There are also programs administered through cereal companies (i.e., BoxTops for Education) that provide money for a designated number of box tops decals collected by school systems. This can be a school project that's easy to facilitate with little effort and time involved.

Numerous grants are also available to enhance school physical education equipment. Some granting agencies are local, while others are state or nationwide. If you would like to seek out grant-funding opportunities, there are several individuals and resources available. Check the NASPE and PE Central web sites for grant opportunities. Sportime and Polar offer additional opportunities for funds to enhance physical education programs, including the latest in technology initiatives and equipment. Many school systems have a grant writer within their central administration office. Grant writers not only can help teachers seek out grants and funding opportunities, but they can assist in the actual task of writing the grant. Be sure to use their expertise to increase the likelihood of being awarded a grant.

Lastly, you may choose to pursue a fundraising activity to provide for additional physical education equipment. Take advantage of opportunities to build your physical education equipment supply. The effort put forth to do so will ultimately benefit your physical education program and students.

School Wellness Programs

As a physical educator, you may wish, at some point in time, to initiate an all-school or a faculty wellness program. There are grants available for this very purpose. Many schools begin by incorporating a jogging/walking program that is conducted during the school day. This can be done before or after school, in addition to lunch or recess time. Health and physical benefits to be gained are numerous. Tracking accumulated laps or miles, and building in a reward incentive program at various levels provides additional motivation for both students and faculty to maintain or improve their current level of physical activity. T-shirts are a great extrinsic reward to offer for a designated amount of miles, etc. Keeping physical activity logs will document progress achieved throughout the program. This project could be designed as an all-out school effort with goals set for each class, in addition to a final school goal to be achieved by the end of the academic year. Initiating this type of program will lend further support to your physical education program through the promotion of daily physical activity.

Intramurals

Intramurals offer another opportunity to increase the amount of physical activity that students receive. These programs are sometimes conducted as an after-school activity. Alternatively, middle schools may build them into their advisory periods, thus providing students with additional physical activity during the actual school day, so that all students are provided the opportunity to participate. Typically, intramural programs provide a variety of physical activities mostly focused on team sports. However, physical educators can create all sorts of competitions and provide a wide array of physical activities. One middle school in my county conducts an annual student-teacher toboggan race. This is done in the southeastern region of the United States without the luxury of snow. A field course is set up on the grassy field area adjacent to the school. Students are positioned on toboggans, while teachers drag the toboggans in a race against one another. Then, roles are reversed. Physical education teachers who design intramural programs are only limited by their level of creativity.

In closing, this chapter provided opportunities for beginning physical education teachers that might be tackled initially, or following the induction phase of their teaching career. Many opportunities exist for physical educators. I challenge you to make the difference in your own physical education program.

Chapter 10

Teaching as a Personal Journey

Physical education was always my favorite subject throughout elementary, middle, and high school years. For the most part, I participated in excellent physical education programs—some cutting edge at the time. Since seventh grade, I knew without a doubt that I wanted to be a physical education teacher. I never changed my mind in terms of a career, although there have been many twists and turns along my journey into teaching.

As I entered the college years, my goal was to become a high school physical education teacher and coach. I planned to do this for the rest of my life. I figured I'd teach and coach at the same high school throughout my entire teaching career. I never imagined that I might be happy teaching at the elementary or middle school levels, and it never crossed my mind that one day I might end up in higher education as a physical education teacher educator.

I accepted my first teaching position three weeks prior to college graduation. What a great feeling it was to know that I didn't have to spend the summer searching for a job. I spent my first two years of teaching at a high school located in a south suburb of Chicago. During that time, I held three coaching positions: varsity girls' gymnastics, assistant boys' gymnastics, and sophomore girls' volleyball. I struggled those first years to teach as I had been taught in my teacher preparation program, and to retain my core teaching values. I feel I was successful at holding on to those philosophical beliefs that were important to me, but it was not an easy road to travel.

I was making good progress in my first teaching position, and was accepted by colleagues, administrators, and students alike as a member of the "school family." When, much to my surprise, I was informed at the end of my second year that I was being RIFed (reduction in force), due in part to a decrease in student enrollment and because I was the most recent hire in the department. I was crushed! This was one of the first "turns" in my personal teaching journey. The job search began again. My remaining years as a public school physical education teacher and coach were spent at a high school and a middle school. I always vowed I would never teach at the middle school level. Recalling my own middle school years I thought, "Who would want to teach kids at that age, anyway?" It was a tough transition from the high school level. Here I was presented another turn in the road on my teaching journey. It surprised me to discover that some of my students were still losing their baby teeth! But, over time, my middle school students grew on me, and taught me much more than I ever imagined possible, in my years as a middle school physical education teacher and coach. Those experiences are often shared with my current students as they prepare to become physical education teachers, and they're also embedded throughout this book.

Roughly seven years into teaching physical education, I decided to begin work on a master's degree in physical education. Mind you, it was the monetary incentive provided by the school district in which I was employed that first motivated me to continue my education. However, that changed over time. Thus began another twist or turn in my teaching journey. I worked full-time, continued with a lighter coaching load, and attended graduate school part-time. I really enjoyed being back in the classroom, which was a surprise since I had sworn I'd never take another course again when I graduated with my bachelor's degree. Although it was overwhelming at times, it was more importantly challenging, invigorating, motivating, and growth-producing.

By the time I completed my master's degree, I was a 10-year teaching veteran (with a couple of maternity leaves built in). My plan was to continue in my current teaching position at the middle school level; however, I contemplated the idea of perhaps teaching at the college level sometime in the future. I came to a fork in the road when that opportunity was presented to me. My recent alma mater offered me first a part-time, then a full-time teaching position in their college of kinesiology. I accepted the offer even though I took a tremendous pay cut in doing so. The position offered new and different challenges, and the opportunity to hopefully impact those who would one day become physical education teachers as well.

Since the start of teaching in higher education, I've worked for three different institutions. At some point during that time, it became evident that should I choose to continue in higher education, it would be necessary to earn a doctorate degree. I made the decision to travel down this pathway in my teaching journey, and 10 years following the attainment of my master's degree, I earned a Ph.D. in Educational Research and Policy Analysis. I still remember my husband urging me to reconsider my decision prior to entering into a doctoral program in which I had no previous experience or education.

However, the decision was intentional on my part. I wanted to create many roads from which I could chose to travel as I entered another phase of my teaching journey. I suspect I'll always be a teacher in whatever position I chose to pursue. Sometime in my future journey as an educator, I anticipate that I will look for administrative opportunities as well.

I will soon embark on my 26th year in the field of education. There have been many bumps and sometimes detours in the journey; however, many roads have led me to places and opportunities I never ventured to imagine! That's what keeps me going strong.

So, what's the moral of this story? Teaching is a journey. To continue on this journey, you will need assistance and support along the way. The journey, in most cases, will not be easy, but instead will be filled with many challenges. The path on which your journey takes you will provide numerous twists and turns. Some of these will be intentional, while others not. There will be times when you encounter a fork in the road, and subsequently will have to make a decision as to which way to proceed. Each individual's teaching journey is unique, and will be impacted by varying contexts, factors, and circumstances. Who knows where your teaching will lead you? Be open for change and ready for the challenges that lay ahead. Stay true to yourself, and always be student-focused. You can change lives one day at a time.

In closing, I'd like to share *A Teacher's Prayer,* by an anonymous author: "One day I would like to teach just a few people many and beautiful things that would help them when they will one day teach a few people." Best wishes as you embark on your teaching journey. Bon voyage!

REFERENCES

Albert, L. (1996). *Cooperative discipline.* Circle Pines, MN: American Guidance Service.

Bain, L., & Wendt, J. (1983). *Transition to teaching: A guide for the beginning teacher.* Reston, VA: AAHPERD.

Campbell, D., Cignetti, P., Melenyzer, B., Nettles, D., & Wyman, R. (1997). *How to develop a professional portfolio: A manual for teachers.* Boston: Allyn and Bacon.

Coleman, L. (1998). Resume advice for educators. In K. Stanley & C. Marshall (Eds.), *1998 job search handbook for educators* (pp. 16-17). Evanston, IL: American Association for Employment in Education.

deCharms, R. (1976). *Enhancing motivation: Change in the classroom.* New York: Irvington.

DePaul, A. (2000). *Survival guide for new teachers: How new teachers can work effectively with veteran teachers, parents, principals, and teacher educators.* Jessup, MD: U.S. Department of Education.

Ellery, P., & Rauschenbach, J. (1997). Developing a professional portfolio. *Strategies, 11*(2), 10-12.

Graham, G., Holt/Hale, S., & Parker, M. (2001). *Children moving: A reflective approach to teaching physical education* (5th ed.). Mountain View, CA: Mayfield.

Hellison, D. (1978). *Beyond balls and bats: Alienated (and other) youth in the gym.* Washington, DC: AAHPERD.

Hellison, D. (1996). Teaching personal and social responsibility. In S. Silverman & C. Ennis (Eds.), *Student learning in physical education: Applying research to enhance instruction* (pp. 269-286). Champaign, IL: Human Kinetics.

Hellison, D. (2003). Teaching personal and social responsibility in physical education. In S. J. Silverman & C. D. Ennis (Eds.), *Student learning in physical education* (2nd. ed., pp. 241-254). Champaign, IL: Human Kinetics.

Metzler, M. (1990). *Instructional supervision for physical education.* Champaign, IL: Human Kinetics.

Metzler, M. (2000). *Instructional models for physical education.* Boston: Allyn and Bacon.

Mohr, D., & Townsend, J. (2001). In the beginning: New physical education teacher's quest for success. *Teaching Elementary Physical Education, 12,* 9-11, 13.

National Association for Sport and Physical Education. (1995). *Moving into the future: National standards for physical education.* Reston, VA: AAHPERD.

Randall, L. (1992). *Handbook for student teaching in physical education.* Champaign, IL: Human Kinetics.

Rikard, G. L., & Senne, T. (1996). A mock interview: Preservice teachers and principals interact. *Journal of Physical Education, Recreation & Dance, 67*(3), 16-17.

Rink, J. (2002). *Teaching physical education for learning* (4th ed.). Boston: McGraw-Hill.

Ryan, S., & Yerg, B. (2001). The effects of crossgroup feedback on off-task behavior in a physical education setting. *Journal of Teaching in Physical Education, 20*(2), 172-188.

Schempp, P., & Graber, K. (1992). Teacher socialization from a dialectical perspective: Pretraining through induction. *Journal of Teaching in Physical Education, 11*(4), 329-348.

Senne, T. (1997). *The interactive teaching portfolio: A developmental approach to promoting professional development in physical education student teachers.* Unpublished doctoral dissertation, North Carolina State University, Raleigh.

Senne, T. (2002a). Transition to teaching: Putting your best foot forward: Part 1. *Journal of Physical Education, Recreation & Dance, 73*(1), 45-49, 53.

Senne, T. (2002b). Transition to teaching: Putting your best foot forward: Part 2. *Journal of Physical Education, Recreation & Dance, 73*(2), 46-52.

Senne, T., & Rikard, G. L. (2002). Experiencing the portfolio process during the internship: A comparative analysis of two PETE portfolio models. *Journal of Teaching in Physical Education, 21*(3), 309-336.

Siedentop, D., & Tannehill, D. (2000). *Developing teaching skills in physical education* (4th ed.). Mountain View, CA: Mayfield.

Simkins, K. (1998). Letters of recommendation. In K. Stanley & C. Marshall (Eds.), *1998 job search handbook for educators* (pp. 18-19). Evanston, IL: American Association for Employment in Education.

Sprinthall, N., Sprinthall, R., & Oja, S. (1994). *Educational psychology: A developmental approach* (6th ed.). New York: McGraw-Hill.

Walberg, H. (1986). Synthesis of research on teaching. In M. C. Wittrock (Ed.), *Handbook of research on teaching* (pp. 214-229). New York: Macmillan.

Wallencheck, E. (1998). Cover letters from start to finish. In K. Stanley & C. Marshall (Eds.), *1998 job search handbook for educators* (pp. 20-21). Evanston, IL: American Association for Employment in Education.

Appendix A

Selected Systematic Observation Instruments

Systematic observation instruments designed by Terry A. Senne:
• BMOI – Behavior Management Observation Instrument
• TMOI – Time Management Observation Instrument
• STSR – Student-Task Success Rate
• MPO – Maximum Practice Opportunities
• PROI – Positive Reinforcement Observation Instrument

Refer to: Metzler, M. (1990). *Instructional supervision for physical education.* Champaign, IL: Human Kinetics for the following systematic observation instruments:
• ALT-PE: Academic Learning Time – PE
• ALT-PEERS: Academic Learning Time – PE Event Recording System

Refer to: Randall, L. (1992). *Handbook for student teaching in physical education.* Champaign, IL: Human Kinetics for the following systematic observation instruments:
• Management Strategies Checklist
• Classroom Management Observation Instrument
• Teaching Cues & Skill-Related Feedback
• Planned Activity Check for Evaluating Lesson Effectiveness (Time on Task)

Refer to: Rink, J. (2002). *Teaching physical education for learning* (4th ed.). Boston: McGraw-Hill for the following systematic observation instruments:
• OSCD-PE: Observation System for Content Development-Physical Education
• QMTPS: Qualitative Measures of Teaching Performance Scale

BMOI
Behavior Management Observation Instrument

Teacher: Date:

Grade Level/Class Period:

Lesson Focus/Activity:

Directions: Record the actual time the lesson started. At the end of class, record the actual time at which the lesson ended. Calculate the length of the observed lesson in minutes and record it under Total Class Time. (Note that this may be different from the designated class period time.) During the lesson, record and briefly describe all episodes of *behavior management* only. Record the duration (minutes/seconds) of each episode to the right of its description. Add the duration of all behavior management episodes to determine Total Behavior Management Time. Calculate percent behavior management using formula provided.

Class started at:_____   Class ended at: _____   Total Class Time: _____

Behavior Management Episodes	Duration
Total Behavior Management Time	

Calculations & Recommendations:

Percent Behavior Management= $\dfrac{\text{Total Behavior Management Time}}{\text{Total Class Time}}$

Percent Behavior Management: _____%
Targeted Percent Behavior Management: _____%

Based on the analyzed data, I need to …

TMOI
TIME MANAGEMENT OBSERVATION INSTRUMENT

Teacher: Date:

Grade Level/Class Period:

Lesson Focus/Activity:

Directions: Record each event (instructional, activity, managerial, other) under the appropriate event category as it occurs during the lesson. Order # designates when the event occurred within the lesson (number as 1, 2, 3, etc.). Record the duration of each event to the right of its description. Once the lesson is over, calculate the total event times for each category, and determine cumulative event time (add all total event times). Calculate percents for each event category using formula provided.

Class started at:_____   Class ended at:_____   Total Class Time:_____

Order #	EVENT (Instructional, Activity, Managerial, Other)	Duration
Instructional Events (cognitive, task explanations, demonstrations, feedback, etc.)		
	Total Instructional Time	
Activity Events (motor-engaged)		
	Total Activity Time	
Managerial Events (organizational aspects of people, equipment, space; transitions)		
	Total Managerial Time	
Other Events (miscellaneous events that do not fit in above categories)		
	Total Other Time	
	CUMULATIVE EVENT TIME	

TMOI (continued)

Calculations & Recommendations:

Percent Event Time = <u>Total Event Category (instructional, activity, managerial, other) Time</u>
Cumulative Event Time

Percent Instructional Time: _____%   *Targeted* Instructional Time: _____%

Percent Activity Time: _____%   *Targeted* Activity Time: _____%

Percent Managerial Time: _____%   *Targeted* Managerial Time: _____%

Percent Other Time: _____%

Based on the analyzed data, I need to …

STSR
STUDENT–TASK SUCCESS RATE

Teacher: Date:
Grade Level/Class Period:
Lesson Focus/Activity:

Directions: Select one high, moderate, and low-skilled student to observe during the lesson. Observe each student for 3-minute intervals sequentially throughout the lesson. Briefly describe the task, and record skill attempts as they occur. Use coding mechanism provided. If the teacher *modifies* the task, record a "TM" at that point and provide a task modification description in the appropriate column. At the lesson conclusion, calculate percent success rates using formula provided.

High-Skilled Student	
Task Description/Modification(s)	**Skill Attempts** (X)=task attempt; XS=successful task attempt; TM=task modification)

Moderate-Skilled Student	
Task Description/Modification(s)	**Skill Attempts** (refer to above coding)

Low-Skilled Student	
Task Description/Modification(s)	**Skill Attempts** (refer to above coding)

STSR (continued)

Calculations & Recommendations:

Percent Success Rate= <u>Total Successful Task Attempts</u>
Total Task Attempts

High-Skilled Student Percent Success Rate: _____%
   Targeted Percent Success Rate: _____%

Moderate-Skilled Student Percent Success Rate: _____%
   Targeted Percent Success Rate: _____%

Low-Skilled Student Percent Success Rate: _____%
   Targeted Percent Success Rate: _____%

*Note: A task is considered *developmentally appropriate* when the learner is able to perform the task at an 80% success rate (Graham et al., 2001).

Based on the analyzed data, I need to …

MPO
MAXIMUM PRACTICE OPPORTUNITIES

Teacher: Date:
Grade Level/Class Period:
Lesson Focus/Activity:

Directions: Provide a brief description of each task as it occurs during the lesson. At the conclusion of each task, use the scoring rubric provided to score how well the task addressed maximum practice opportunities. Record score to the right of task description. At the lesson conclusion, calculate average maximum practice opportunities using formula provided.

Scoring Rubric:

1 point	Wait time is evident. **Few** students are actively engaged in practice.
2 points	**Some** students are actively engaged in practice.
3 points	**Most** students are actively engaged in practice.
4 points	**All** students are actively engaged in practice.

Task Description	Score
CUMULATIVE SCORE	

Calculations & Recommendations:

Average Maximum Practice Opportunities = $\dfrac{\text{Cumulative Score}}{\text{Total \# of Tasks}}$

Average Maximum Practice Opportunities: _____

Targeted Average Maximum Practice Opportunities: _____

Based on the analyzed data, I need to …

PROI
POSITIVE REINFORCEMENT OBSERVATION INSTRUMENT

Teacher: Date:
Grade Level/Class Period:
Lesson Focus/Activity:

Directions: Select desired category pairs (male/female, high-skilled/low-skilled, etc.) and write them in the designated space provided at top of category columns. Record each reinforcement statement/cue (verbal, nonverbal, differentiated, delayed) provided by the teacher under the appropriate reinforcement type. Refer to PROI page 2 for descriptions. Record the frequency rate of each reinforcement statement/cue using a tally mark to indicate each occurrence in the designated category column. At lesson conclusion, calculate data using formulas provided. Record results in Data Summary Table.

Reinforcement Type:		
Verbal Reinforcement	Category A Tally #'s	Category B Tally #'s
Total Verbal Reinforcement Tallies		
Nonverbal Reinforcement	Category A Tally #'s	Category B Tally #'s
Total Nonverbal Reinforcement Tallies		
Differentiated Reinforcement	Category A Tally #'s	Category B Tally #'s
Total Differentiated Reinforcement Tallies		
Delayed Reinforcement	Category A Tally #'s	Category B Tally #'s
Total Delayed Reinforcement Tallies		
CUMULATIVE REINFORCEMENT TALLIES		

PROI (continued)

Reinforcement Category Descriptions

Verbal Reinforcement: When a student answers a question correctly or asks a good question, does the teacher reward with words such as "Excellent," "Great," "Super," "Terrific," and provide a reason for the reinforcement ("Excellent thinking," "Great idea," "Super question," "Terrific response")?

Nonverbal Reinforcement: Does the teacher use nonverbal cues (smiles, nods approvingly, thumbs up, high five, etc.) to encourage students?

Differentiated Reinforcement: When a student gives a _partially_ correct response, does the teacher give credit for that which was correct?

Delayed Reinforcement: Does the teacher ever refer to the positive aspects of a student's previous response ("One point Jake made that I thought was very observant was….")? This type of reinforcement is the most potent of all reinforcement categories.

Calculations & Recommendations:

Percent Reinforcement Type (verbal, nonverbal, differentiated, or delayed) is calculated as follows:

Total Designated Reinforcement Type (verbal, nonverbal, differentiated, or delayed) Tallies
Total Cumulative Reinforcement Tallies

Total Designated Reinforcement Type Tallies is calculated as follows:

Category A tallies + Category B tallies for designated reinforcement type

Total Cumulative Reinforcement Tallies is calculated as follows:

Category A cumulative reinforcement tallies + Category B cumulative reinforcement tallies

Percent Category A or B Reinforcement Type is calculated as follows:

Category A or B tallies for designated reinforcement type
Total Designated Reinforcement Type Tallies

Data Summary Table

Reinforcement Type	Category A%	Category B%	Total %
Verbal Reinforcement			
Nonverbal Reinforcement			
Differentiated Reinforcement			
Delayed Reinforcement			

Based on the analyzed data, I need to …

APPENDIX B:

SELECTED RESOURCES FOR PHYSICAL EDUCATORS

Assessment

- Doolittle, S., & Fay, T. (2002). *Authentic assessment of physical activity for high school students.* Reston, VA: National Association for Sport and Physical Education [NASPE].
- Holt/Hale, S. (1999). *Assessing and improving fitness in elementary physical e education.* Reston, VA: NASPE.
- Holt/Hale, S. (1999). *Assessing motor skills in elementary physical education.* Reston, VA: NASPE.
- Lambert, L. (1999). *Standards-based assessment of student learning.* Reston, VA: NASPE.
- Lund, J. (2000). *Creating rubrics for physical education.* Reston, VA: NASPE.
- Lund, J., & Kirk, M. (2002). *Performance-based assessment for middle and high school physical education.* Champaign, IL: Human Kinetics.
- Melograno, V. (2000). *Portfolio assessment for K-12 physical education.* Reston, VA: NASPE.
- Mitchell, S., & Oslin, J. (1999). *Assessment in games teaching.* Reston, VA: NASPE.
- O'Sullivan, M., & Henninger, M. (2000). *Assessing student responsibility and teamwork.* Reston, VA: NASPE.

Classroom Management

- Albert, L. (1996). *Cooperative discipline.* Circle Pines, MN: American Guidance Service.
- Clark, R. (2003). *The essential 55 – An award-winning educator's rules for discovering the successful student in every child.* New York: Hyperion.
- Hellison, D. (1995). *Teaching responsibility through physical activity.* Champaign, IL: Human Kinetics.
- Lavay, B., French, R., & Henderson, H. (1997). *Positive behavior management for physical educators.* Champaign, IL: Human Kinetics.
- PE Central. *Creating a positive climate for learning.* Retrieved May 14, 2003, from http://www.pecentral.org/climate/index.html

Curriculum

- Hopple, C. (1995). *Teaching for outcomes in elementary physical education: A guide for curriculum and assessment.* Champaign, IL: Human Kinetics.
- Jewett, A., Bain, L., & Ennis, C. (1995). *The curriculum process in physical education* (2nd ed.). Madison, WI: WCB Brown & Benchmark.
- Lambert, L. (1996). Goals and objectives. In S. Silverman & C. Ennis (Eds.), *Student learning in physical education: Applying research to enhance instruction* (pp. 149-170). Champaign, IL: Human Kinetics.
- Melograno, V. (1996). *Designing the physical education curriculum* (3rd ed.). Champaign, IL: Human Kinetics.
- National Association for Sport and Physical Education [NASPE]. (1995). *Moving into the future: National standards for physical education.* Reston, VA: AAHPERD.
- Rink, J. (2002). *Teaching physical education for learning* (4th ed.). Boston: McGraw-Hill.
- Siedentop, D., & Tannehill, D. (2000). *Developing teaching skills in physical education* (4th ed.). Mountain View, CA: Mayfield.

Instructional Planning

- Graham, G., Holt/Hale, S., & Parker, M. (2004). *Children moving: A reflective approach to teaching physical education* (6th ed.). Boston: McGraw-Hill.
- Harrison, J., Blakemore, C., Buck, M., & Pellett, T. (1996). *Instructional strategies for secondary school physical education* (4th ed.). Chicago: Brown & Benchmark.
- Hastie, P. (2003). *Teaching for lifetime physical activity through quality high school physical education.* San Francisco: Benjamin Cummings.
- Metzler, M. (2000). *Instructional models for physical education.* Boston: Allyn and Bacon.
- Mohnsen, B. (2003a). (Ed.). *Concepts and principles of physical education: What every student needs to know* (2nd ed.). Reston, VA: NASPE.
- Mohnsen, B. (2003b). *Teaching middle school physical education: A standards-based approach for grades 5-8* (2nd ed.). Champaign, IL: Human Kinetics.
- NASPE. (1998). *Appropriate practices for high school physical education.* Reston, VA: Author.
- NASPE. (2000). *Appropriate practices for elementary school physical education.* Reston, VA: Author.
- NASPE. (2001). *Appropriate practices for middle school physical education.* Reston, VA: Author.
- Rink, J. (2002). *Teaching physical education for learning* (4th ed.). Boston: McGraw-Hill.
- Siedentop, D., & Tannehill, D. (2000). *Developing teaching skills in physical*

education (4th ed.). Mountain View, CA: Mayfield.

Physical Activities

- Dougherty, N. (Ed.). (2002). *Physical activity and sport for the secondary school student* (5th ed.). Reston, VA: NASPE.
- Ermler, K., & Mehrhof, J. (1996). *Ideas III: Middle school physical activities for a fit generation.* Reston, VA: NASPE.
- Graham, G., Holt/Hale, S., & Parker, M. (2004). *Children moving: A reflective approach to teaching physical education* (6th ed.). Boston: McGraw-Hill.
- Mood, D., Musker, F., & Rink, J. (2003). *Sports and recreational activities* (13th ed.). Boston: McGraw-Hill.
- Philipp, J., & Wilkerson, J. (1990). *Teaching team sports: A coeducational approach.* Champaign, IL: Human Kinetics.
- Schmottlach, N., & McManama, J. (2002). *Physical education activity handbook* (10th ed.). San Francisco: Benjamin Cummings.
- Sherrill, C. (1998). *Adapted physical activity, recreation and sport: Cross disciplinary and lifespan* (5th ed.). Boston: WCB McGraw-Hill.
- Winnick, J. (Ed.). (2000). *Adapted physical education and sport.* Champaign, IL: Human Kinetics.
- Zakrajsek, D., Carnes, L., & Pettigrew, F. (2003). *Quality lesson plans for secondary physical education* (2nd ed.). Champaign, IL: Human Kinetics.

Physical Education Websites

- NASPE—http://www.naspeinfo.org/
- PE Central—http://pecentral.org/
- P.E.4Life—http://www.pe4life.org/
- Sportime—http://www.sportime.com/index.jsp

Physical Fitness

- American Alliance for Health, Physical Education, Recreation and Dance (AAHPERD). (1999). *Physical best activity guide: Elementary level.* Champaign, IL: Human Kinetics.
- AAHPERD. (1999). *Physical best activity guide: Secondary level.* Champaign, IL: Human Kinetics.
- AAHPERD. (1999). *Physical education for lifelong fitness.* Champaign, IL: Human Kinetics.

Teaching Approaches/Instructional Models

- Butler, J., Griffin, L., Lombardo, B., & Nastasi, R. (Eds.). (2003). *Teaching games for understanding in physical education and sport: An international perspective*. Reston, VA: NASPE.
- Metzler, M. (2000). *Instructional models for physical education*. Boston: Allyn and Bacon.
- Mosston, M., & Ashworth, S. (2002). *Teaching physical education* (5th ed.). San Francisco: Benjamin Cummings.
- Rink, J. (2002). *Teaching physical education for learning* (4th ed.). Boston: McGraw-Hill.
- Siedentop, D., & Tannehill, D. (2000). *Developing teaching skills in physical education* (4th ed.). Mountain View, CA: Mayfield.

Teaching/Coaching Conflict

- Carpenter, J. (1996). Teacher-coaches speak out. *Teaching Secondary Physical Education, 2*(6), 10-11.
- Cash, S. (1996). Tips for new teacher-coaches. *Teaching Secondary Physical Education, 2*(6), 20.
- Darst, P., & Pangrazi, R. (1996). The teaching/coaching challenge. *Teaching Secondary Physical Education, 2*(6), 4-5.
- Drake, D., & Hebert, E. (2002). Perceptions of occupational stress and strategies for avoiding burnout: Case studies of two female teacher-coaches. *Physical Educator, 59*(4), 170-183.
- Morford, L. (1996). Coping with teacher-coach conflict. *Teaching Secondary Physical Education, 2*(6), 6-7.
- Wirszyla, C. (2002). State-mandated curriculum change in three high school physical education programs. *Journal of Teaching in Physical Education, 22*(1), 4-19.

Technology

- Kirkpatrick, B., & Birnbaum, B. (1997). *Lessons from the heart: Individualizing physical education with heart rate monitors*. Champaign, IL: Human Kinetics.
- Mohnsen, B. (2001). *Using technology in physical education* (3rd ed.). Reston, VA: NASPE.

The American Alliance for Health, Physical Education, Recreation and Dance

JOIN TODAY, AND PUT AAHPERD TO WORK FOR YOU!

AAHPERD Membership Application

☐ **YES**, I want to join AAHPERD. Please send my Association credentials, and begin my subscription to Update and the professional journal(s) I've checked below.

(Mr.) (Ms.) (Dr.)
Name _____

Please fill out both addresses below and then tell us which one you'd like to use.

1. Business/Academic Address

Place of Employment _____

Address _____

City _____ State _____ Zip _____

Work Phone _____ Fax _____

E-mail _____

2. Home Address

Address _____

City _____ State _____ Zip _____

Home Phone _____

Preferred Membership Mailing Address
☐ Business/Academic ☐ Home

Your satisfaction is 100% guaranteed.
Cancel any time and you'll receive a full
refund on all the months remaining on
your membership. *Join AAHPERD*
with confidence!

Customize your membership

Choose your Associations
AAHPERD membership includes membership in any two Associations. Please prioritize your choices. Students may join only one Association.

1 2 American Association for Active Lifestyles and Fitness
1 2 American Association for Health Education
1 2 American Association for Leisure and Recreation
1 2 National Association for Girls and Women in Sport
1 2 National Association for Sport and Physical Education
1 2 National Dance Association
☐ **Research Consortium** For those interested in research. (Select this in addition to your association affiliation(s) at no extra charge to you.)

Choose your Professional Journals
☐ *Journal of Physical Education, Recreation & Dance*
☐ *American Journal of Health Education*
☐ *Research Quarterly for Exercise and Sport*
☐ *Strategies*
You receive a subscription to one professional journal with your membership in AAHPERD. Subscriptions to additional journals are only $25 each per year.

Figure your dues
AAHPERD Professional Membership
OR ($125 per year) $ _____
AAHPERD Student Membership*
($45 per year) $ _____
Additional Professional Journals
($25 per year) $ _____
Foreign Postage *(Outside U.S. & Canada* $ _____
add $8 per journal including Update.)
TOTAL DUE $ _____

*Proof of full-time student status required. Please attach photocopy of current student ID or other proof.

Payment Options
☐ My check is enclosed for a full year's Membership.
☐ Please charge my ☐ VISA ☐ MASTERCARD ☐ AMEX
    ☐ Annual Payment ☐ Quarterly Payment*

Card No. ☐☐☐☐☐☐☐☐☐☐☐☐☐☐☐☐☐☐☐

Expiration Date: _____

Signature: _____

*Quarterly payments (credit card only) renew automatically until canceled by you.

For Office Use Only
DepDt: _____
Ck #: _____
Amt: _____

American Alliance for Health, Physical Education, Recreation and Dance
1900 Association Drive, Reston, VA 20191-1598
Phone: 800-213-7193 • Fax: 703-476-9527 • membership@aahperd.org • http://www.aahperd.org

MIAP

SUBJECT INDEX

Communication
  parents 73-75
  public relations and advocacy 76-77
  school personnel 75
  students 69-73
Community 85-86, *See also* Socialization factors
  cultivating connections and collaboration 104
Conferences and workshops *See* Professional development
Consequences *See* Classroom management
Continuing education *See* Professional development
Cover letter 4-6

D

Development plan *See* Professional development

E

Equipment/equipment room 61-62, *See also* Facilities
  enhancing of 105-106

F

Facilities
  equipment room 61-62
  gymnasium 60
  indoor 60
  locker room 61
  office 60-61
  outdoor 62

G

Goals *See* Professional development
Grade book example *See* Record keeping
Gymnasium and indoor facilities *See* Facilities

H

Health education
  classroom 104-105
  lesson plans, links, and resources 105

I

Indoor facilities *See* Facilities
INTASC standards 94-95
Interview strategies and guidelines
  administrator interview questions 18-19, 21
  information 24
  interview 19-21
  pre-interview 17-19
  post-interview 21
  teacher candidate interview questions 21-22
Intramurals 107

J

Job application process 11-15
  contact summary worksheet 14
Job search techniques
  classifieds 23
  job fairs 22-24
  Internet 23-24
  networking 22-23

L

Liability 53, 67
Locker room 30-31, *See also* Facilities

M

Maintaining balance
  common sense stuff 101-102
  teaching/coaching conflict 99-100

R

S

RESOURCES

Published by the National Association for Sport and Physical Education for quality physical education programs:

Moving Into the Future: National Standards for Physical Education, A Guide to Content, 2nd edition. (2004), Stock No. 304-10275

Concepts and Principles of Physical Education: What Every Student Needs to Know (2003), Stock No. 304-10261

Beyond Activities: Elementary Volume (2003), Stock No. 304-10265

Beyond Activities: Secondary Volume (2003), Stock No. 304-10268

National Physical Education Standards in Action (2003), 304-10267

Physical Activity for Children: A Statement of Guidelines (2004), Stock No. 304-10276

National Standards for Beginning Physical Education Teachers (2003), Stock No. 304-10273

Active Start: A Statement of Physical Activity Guidelines for Children Birth to Five Years (2002), Stock No. 304-10254

Appropriate Practice Documents

Appropriate Practice in Movement Programs for Young Children, (2000), Stock No. 304-10232

Appropriate Practices for Elementary School Physical Education (2000), Stock No. 304-10230

Appropriate Practices for Middle School Physical Education (2001), Stock No. 304-10248

Appropriate Practices for High School Physical Education (2004), Stock No. 304-10272

Opportunity to Learn Documents

Opportunity to Learn Standards for Elementary Physical Education (2000), Stock No. 304-10242

Physical Education Program Improvement and Self-Study Guides (1998) for Middle School, Stock No. 304-10173, for High School, Stock No. 304-10174

Assessment Series

Assessment in Outdoor Adventure Physical Education (2003), Stock No. 304-10218

Assessing Student Outcomes in Sport Education (2003), Stock No. 304-10219

Video Tools for Teaching Motor Skill Assessment (2002), Stock No. 304-10217

Assessing Heart Rate in Physical Education (2002), Stock No. 304-10214

Authentic Assessment of Physical Activity for High School Students (2002), Stock No. 304-10216

Portfolio Assessment for K-12 Physical Education (2000), Stock No. 304-10213

Elementary Heart Health: Lessons and Assessment (2001), Stock No. 304-10215

Standards-Based Assessment of Student Learning: A Comprehensive Approach (1999), Stock No. 304-10206

Assessment in Games Teaching (1999), Stock No. 304-10212

Assessing Motor Skills in Elementary Physical Education (1999), Stock No. 304-10207

Assessing and Improving Fitness in Elementary Physical Education (1999), Stock No. 304-10208

Creating Rubrics for Physical Education (1999), Stock No. 304-10209

Assessing Student Responsibility and Teamwork (1999), Stock No. 304-10210

Preservice Professional Portfolio System (1999), Stock No. 304-10211

Order online at www.aahperd.org/naspe or **call 1-800-321-0789**

Shipping and handling additional.

National Association for Sport and Physical Education

an association of the American Alliance for
Health, Physical Education, Recreation and Dance

1900 Association Drive • Reston, VA 20191

naspe@aahperd.org • 703-476-3410 • www.naspeinfo.org